PENGUIN
SAHIBS WHO L

Khushwant Singh is India's best-known writer and columnist. He has been founder-editor of *Yojana* and editor of the *Illustrated Weekly of India*, the *National Herald* and the *Hindustan Times*. He is the author of classics such as *Train to Pakistan*, *I Shall Not Hear the Nightingale* and *Delhi*. His latest novel, *The Sunset Club*, written when he was 95, was published by Penguin Books in 2010. His non-fiction includes the classic two-volume *A History of the Sikhs*, a number of translations and works on Sikh religion and culture, Delhi, nature, current affairs and Urdu poetry. His autobiography, *Truth, Love and a Little Malice*, was published by Penguin Books in 2002.

Khushwant Singh was a member of Parliament from 1980 to 1986. He was awarded the Padma Bhushan in 1974 but returned the decoration in 1984 in protest against the storming of the Golden Temple in Amritsar by the Indian Army. In 2007, he was awarded the Padma Vibhushan.

Among the other awards he has received are the Punjab Ratan, the Sulabh International award for the most honest Indian of the year, and honorary doctorates from several universities. He passed away in 2014 at the age of 99.

SAHIBS WHO LOVED INDIA

Compiled and Edited by
KHUSHWANT SINGH

PENGUIN BOOKS

PENGUIN BOOKS

USA | Canada | UK | Ireland | Australia
New Zealand | India | South Africa | China

Penguin Books is part of the Penguin Random House group of companies
whose addresses can be found at global.penguinrandomhouse.com

Published by Penguin Random House India Pvt. Ltd
7th Floor, Infinity Tower C, DLF Cyber City,
Gurgaon 122 002, Haryana, India

First published in Viking by Penguin Books India 2008
Published in Penguin Books 2010

12 11 10 9 8 7 6 5

ISBN 9780143415800

Typeset in Perpetua by InoSoft Systems, Noida

Printed at Repro Knowledgecast Limited, India

www.penguin.co.in

Contents

～

PREFACE

~

SOMETIME IN FEBRUARY this year, my son Rahul, who lives in Mumbai, redirected a bound manuscript of articles I had commissioned over thirty years ago for the now defunct *Illustrated Weekly of India*. The man who had sent it was Phillip Knightley, once editor of *The Sunday Times* of London. He was not sure whether or not I was still around, so he sent it to my son to do whatever he wanted with it.

When I was editor of the *Illustrated Weekly*, I had invited English men and women who had lived in India after Independence to write on 'What India Meant to Me'. Amongst those who had responded were Lord Mountbatten, members of the Indian Civil Service, journalists, boxwallahs, housewives and others. I went over the essays again and found them fascinating as well as relevant to our times.

For far too long, we have looked upon the English as unwanted rulers who exploited India, kept their distance from Indians, and as soon as their tenures were over, went back to their homes in England and were happy to forget the time they spent in this country. This lopsided image of the English in India persists in the minds of most Indians. It is true that the majority of those who came here came because they could not get good jobs in their own country. They hated everything about India: its climate, mosquitoes, flies, the filth, dirt and smell. Above all, they hated Indians. There were others who enjoyed the luxury of living in spacious bungalows with servants, shikar, riding, pig-sticking, drinking, dancing... but even they kept themselves aloof from Indians with their 'Whites Only' clubs.

However, there was a third variety that liked everything about India, stayed away from the racist clubs, went out of their way to befriend Indians and maintained contacts with them after returning to England. Some even lent tacit support to the freedom movement and stayed on in India after the country gained independence, reluctantly returning to England when their bread-winners retired. I was fortunate in knowing quite a few of this breed—both those I befriended during my long years in England and those I got to know in India—Sinbad Sinclair, Evan Charlton, Henry Croom-Johnson, Guy Wint, Naomi Mitchison, Kingsley Martin, Dorothy Norman, Susan Hickling, Elizabeth Spillius (née Bott), the Lyons, the Harwoods and Edmund and Celia Leach, to name a few. Whenever any one of them visited Delhi, they stayed with me. Whenever I went to England, I stayed with one of them in London or Oxford.

Amongst the closest to me were the Sinclairs. Sinbad was head of Burmah Shell. When in Bombay, I did not stay in a hotel or with an Indian friend, but with Elinor Sinclair and her family. Later, whenever I was in England, the Sinclairs' home in London was my home. Sinbad died quite some time ago. I can never forget his description of his last meeting with Pandit Gobind Ballabh Pant to settle terms of the takeover of Burmah Shell by the Indian Government. Both men suffered from Parkinson's disease and their hands shook while holding the draft of the agreement in their fingers.

Guy Wint was the next to go. He had a stroke in the train on his way from Oxford to spend the weekend with me in London. I spent one summer with his wife Freda and their two children in their home in Oxford. Freda converted to Buddhism. She would have been ninety-six if she were here today.

Henry Croom-Johnson went about ten years ago; his wife followed a few months after he did. Henry had been the head of the British Council. His wife, Jane, a tall, handsome, grey-eyed blonde, made it a point to reach out to Indians. She stayed with me in Kasauli. My daughter Mala and I stayed with her in London.

Only Elinor Sinclair, who was the same age as I, remained. I was told her memory was fast failing. However, when I had called on her in London in 2000, I noticed no lapse of memory. She asked about every member of my family, had me autograph books I had sent her and told me she was writing her Indian memoirs. In 2004, I wrote to her from Kasauli and got no reply. I concluded she too had deserted me. But that was not so. I learnt that her daughter Margaret, who looked after her, had responded but her letter never reached me. Later that year, Sinbad's son Mark rang me up from London to tell me he would be spending an evening with me and that he'd bring a copy of Margaret's letter. So he did. It said Elinor was in poor shape. Her memory was gone, she was confined to a wheelchair. Margaret also mentioned that Joy Charlton, who had been in good health, had suddenly died while she was at work. *The Statesman*, which her husband Evan had edited for many years in Delhi and Calcutta, did not carry a word about her going. It was a long evening by the fireside. Mark, who looks the spitting image of his father from the snow-white mop of hair down to his toes, has his mother's intonation. He went down the list of obituaries. I felt deserted and recalled lines from Thomas Moore's 'Oft, in the Stilly Night': *When I remember all / The friends so linked together, / I've seen around me fall, / Like leaves in wintry weather; / I feel like one / Who treads alone / Some banquet-hall, deserted, / Whose lights are fled, / Whose garlands dead, / And all, but he, departed!*

Now, with Elinor gone, only their memories linger. I felt I owed it to my close English friends to record not only what India, but also Indians, meant to them.

～

I DEDICATE THIS BOOK TO THE LOVING MEMORY OF ELINOR SINCLAIR WHO DIED IN LONDON ON 19 APRIL 2005.

KHUSHWANT SINGH
NEW DELHI
JUNE 2008

I

What India Meant to Me

~

LORD MOUNTBATTEN OF BURMA

During the 200 years of our British 'connection', many proconsuls have held sway over India. Lord Mountbatten was one of those who erased the memory of Clive, Hastings and General Dyer.

K.S.
24 January 1971

ON 17 NOVEMBER 1921, the Prince of Wales arrived on board the great battle cruiser, *Renown*, in Bombay for his Indian tour. I was one of his Royal Highness's ADCs, being at that time a twenty-one-year-old naval lieutenant. The tour lasted until 17 March 1922, when we re-embarked on board *HMS Renown* at Karachi.

During this time we visited Poona, Baroda, Rutlam, Udaipur, Ajmer, Jodhpur, Bikaner, Bharatpur, Lucknow, Allahabad, Banares, Nepal, Patna, Calcutta, Madras, Bangalore, Mysore, Karapur, Hyderabad, Secunderabad, Nagpur, Indore, Mhow, Bhopal, Kachnaria, Gwalior, Agra, Delhi, Patiala, Jullundur, Lahore, Jammu, Sialkot, Jhelum, Peshawar, Kyber Pass, Mardan, Malakhand, Chakdara, Risalpur, Nowshera, Taxila, Rawalpindi, Kapurthala, and finally, Karachi.

I have given this list to show how very extensively the Royal party travelled all over India. During these four months we really covered practically the whole of India and I must confess I immediately fell in love with the country.

However, there was a special reason why India had an additional warm spot in my heart because, while we were in Delhi staying at the old, temporary Viceregal Lodge, a beautiful young girl of whom I had become very fond in England had come out to stay with the Viceroy, Lord Reading. Her name was Edwina Ashley and on 14 February 1922, during a dance in the house, I sat out with her during the fifth dance in a small sitting room and proposed marriage to her. She accepted me and all my happiness started from that day.

The Prince of Wales was delighted and most helpful. I had to have the King's permission to marry and he saw to all that. Later I discovered there had only been one really dissenting voice when we announced our engagement—the Vicereine's, Lady Reading, who wrote to Edwina's aunt and said: 'I am afraid she has definitely made up her mind about him. I hoped she would have cared for someone older, with more of a career before him.'

Thus we both were tied to India with every possible bond of memory and affection, which clearly played an important part in our lives when I came out again in 1947 as the last Viceroy and indeed when I stayed on as the first Governor-General of the independent country of India.

A curious thing happened a quarter of a century later. On 7 March 1948, I presided at the Silver Jubilee convocation of the University of Delhi. During this we conferred honorary degrees on the most eminent men of India and in particular, upon Pandit Jawaharlal Nehru.

In my speech I said: 'It is a curious, but to my wife and myself a very pleasant coincidence that Delhi University should be celebrating the Silver Jubilee of its foundation in 1922; for we were married in that year and have just celebrated our Silver Wedding. The connection between these two events may not be immediately apparent until I tell you that the room in which I asked my wife to marry me in February 1922 was Room No. 13, which is now the Registrar's Office. I am afraid I cannot claim that we were both members of the University, for the University at that time had not been founded, and the building in which the proposal took place was then the Viceregal Lodge.'

MEETING GANDHIJI

Mahatma Gandhi was in Bombay when we arrived in 1921. I was curious about him—he was always a remarkable figure —and I tried to contrive for him to meet the Prince, who was quite keen on the idea. But the Government of India was against it. I then asked if I might meet Gandhi myself, but the answer was 'no'. The government didn't really want any contact at all. I have often wondered since whether a meeting would have done any good as we might have established a useful contact. Even if the Prince of Wales had not been allowed to meet him it would have been great help to me if I had been allowed to meet him, particularly in view of the friendship we made when I got to know him finally in 1947.

In the diary I kept at the time I noted how friendly was the reception which we had from the people everywhere, except in Allahabad. We arrived here on 12 December. It was the first private arrival, that is to say, there were no Guards of

Honour and lounge suits were worn; the streets were for the first, and really only, time of our tour almost deserted.

I think it was then that I realized how intensely the Indian leaders felt about acquiring independence. So I got the feeling of this at first-hand a good quarter of a century before I actually came out as the last Viceroy to transfer power.

I must admit that I was deeply struck by the devotion to India of the British members of the Indian Civil Service. They were unanimous in their expressions of real love for the country and the people. There may have been cases of unfortunate behaviour but I must confess that I never came across any in those days.

So I came away after my four months' tour, during which I had become engaged to be married, with a lasting love of India and her people.

When, in October 1943, I set up the Supreme Allied Command in South-East Asia, I had close on a million Indian sailors, soldiers and airmen serving under me. I was particularly proud of this and admired their courage and steadfastness. They certainly fought magnificently and made a great international reputation for themselves.

Thus when I finally came out as Viceroy I could add to my feeling of twenty-five years before of love for the country my two and a half years' association with so many Indian fighting men in the war.

No wonder it was easy to feel a real happiness at being back in India, in the country my wife and I had grown to love, among the people we admired and liked so much.

It was a wonderful experience when the people of India on all levels appeared to return our feeling so that the whole of our time in India from beginning to end was one of real happiness in spite of the many difficulties which had to be overcome.

So 'What India Meant to Me' can be summed up in one phrase, 'Fascination, affection and happiness'.

~

LOUIS FRANCIS ALBERT VICTOR NICHOLAS GEORGE MOUNTBATTEN, First Earl Mountbatten of Burma, British admiral and statesman, was the last Viceroy and the first Governor-General of independent India. He died in 1979 at the age of 79.

II

India Educated Me

~

ESCOTT REID

INDIA IS MY ALMA MATER, the university of my middle age. Part of a liberal education consists in gaining a better understanding of the world we live in. I find the world increasingly difficult to understand but I would find it much more difficult if I had not been educated by the experience of four and a half years in India.

India opened for me a window on the two-thirds of the world which is separated from the North Atlantic community—in which I spent the first forty-seven years of my life—by poverty, by colour, by culture, by religion, by ways of life.

I saw something in India of what the poverty of two-thirds of the world is like and it is difficult for a Westerner to comprehend the depth of this poverty unless he has seen it with his own eyes.

I came to appreciate the magnitude of the difficulties which the governments and people of India confront in the struggle against evils so various, so numerous, so intractable and so monstrous—the evils of hunger, illiteracy, disease and ignorance, of feudalism, social inequality, casteism and communalism, the evils of superstition and of obscurantism. I knew that other poor countries faced similar difficulties.

The four-month-long hot season of Delhi helped me to realize how heavy is the toll which so many poor countries pay to the tyranny of the tropics, a toll described by Rabindranath Tagore as 'the heat, the damp, the unspeakable fecundity of minute life feeding upon big life, the perpetual sources of irritation, visible and invisible.'

India educated me into realizing that by far the most important task of man in our times is to speed up the dangerously slow rate of the economic and social advance of the poor two-thirds of mankind.

I knew that if the rich nations were to be persuaded to give aid in sufficient volume, their governments would have to be able to convince legislatures and voters that the aid which they were paying for out of their taxes was not being misused.

I also knew that for a rich nation to give advice to a poor nation on how that nation should run its own affairs is a difficult and a hazardous operation, especially since it is only proud nations which are worth helping.

This led me to draft, when I was with the World Bank in Washington, the following statement of some of the things which experience in India had convinced me that international advisers to poor countries should constantly keep in mind: Human judgement is fallible. Luck or providence or the unpredictable plays a large role in economic development. While it is a good thing for poor people to have more to eat and wear, better places to live in, more and better nurses, doctors and teachers, and less illness, it is a better thing for them to have these goods without sacrificing those ancient values of their society which can give them a feeling of belonging to a group, a sense of dignity, and the possibility of serenity. The success of an international adviser is measured not by the wisdom of the advice he gives but by how much of his wise advice is accepted. His task is one of persuasion. When he intervenes with advice his 'intervention should be in the least abrasive, the least corrosive way possible'.

My alma mater, India, has also helped me with another part of a liberal education, that part which 'consists in breaking the influence of the world we live in and finding deliverance from the tyranny of the immediate, the novel and the transitory'.

The experience of beauty, the memories of beauty, these are ways of deliverance and I cherish my memories of the heartbreaking beauty of India—in the plains and in the mountains, at ancient monuments and at holy shrines.

I often think back on the first tour of the Indian countryside which my wife and our daughter and I made a few months after we had arrived in India. My memories are full of colour, of fragrance and of music. The golden glow of the early morning and the late afternoon. The gold of the mustard fields. The fragrance of the flowering fields of peas and mustard. The tree-lined canal banks, the long shadows of late afternoon and early morning. The bells of the bullock-carts. And the gay singing of the villagers heard across the fields during the day or from the villages at night.

It was in India that I first read Edward Thompson's *The Youngest Disciple* and I can sometimes find escape from the transitory in this inspired rendering of the teachings of the Buddha whom Jawaharlal Nehru delighted to call India's greatest son. I felt closer to the Buddha and his teachings after I had been to the Vulture's Peak.

From time to time I try my hand at piecing together from various translations of the *Bhagavad Gita* my own personal version of bits of it, especially the requiem, which I heard B.K. Nehru, then ambassador in Washington, read at the memorial service to Jawaharlál Nehru in the Anglican Cathedral in Washington: 'The wise mourn not for those who live and they mourn not for those who die, for life and death shall pass away. Invisible before birth are all beings and after death invisible again. They are seen between two unseens. What is there in this for lamentation?'

India means to me memories of my calls every week or two on Raghavan Pillai, the brilliant, devoted secretary-general of the external affairs ministry who honoured me with his friendship—and the movies which we and our wives used to go to together. It means memories of innumerable talks on common problems with ministers and civil servants. We argued, we differed, but because our talks—unlike so many diplomatic discussions—were really full and frank and free, we were able to help our two countries to accomplish together something for peace, notably in Korea, Indo-China and the Suez Canal and to accomplish together something in that pioneer venture, the Colombo Plan.

And India means to me memories of Jawaharlal Nehru. I remember his elegance, his charm as host or guest, his stream-of-consciousness speeches, occasionally dull, but usually illuminating and moving. I remember the way in which he revelled in the endless adventure of politics, revelled in whirling, restless, relentless activity, the activity of the creative, practical politician who conceived his task to be to prod, push, pull, cajole, lead India out of the bullock-cart and cow-dung age into the age of jet airplanes and nuclear energy.

I remember his many personal kindnesses to me. A diplomat who has had the privilege of knowing one of the great men of his time is one on whom fortune has smiled. Fortune smiled on me from 1952 to 1957.

~

ESCOTT MEREDITH REID was a Canadian diplomat, author, international public servant and academic administrator. He joined the Canadian Foreign Service in 1939 and was the High Commissioner for Canada to India from 1952 to 1957. He died in 1999.

III

The Splendour of India

~

ROWLAND OWEN

IT IS NOW OVER twenty years since I left India. My period of
serving as Senior British Trade Commissioner, residing in
Delhi, bracketed a period of political and economic
reconstruction which strained to the limit the ingenuity and
resources of India's political leaders and her public service,
and which made far from easy the task of external observers
in attempting to follow the influences and ideas which were
to launch a great new country on newly independent paths.

It had always been my wish, indeed my ambition, to serve
in India, and when, after the war, the opportunity came to
assume the post, I felt that there was an element of destiny
about it. I knew it was going to mean the assumption of a
tremendous task, but the prospect of participating
constructively in impending drastic changes in Indo-British
relations, after a somewhat frustrating spell in economic aspects
of war administration, was both stimulating and challenging.
Looking back on it now, and re-reading my final report on
India in 1952, I still recall vividly the stimulus and the
excitement of an assignment which gave me more satisfaction
than any other in a lifetime of public service.

THE WAR YEARS

As in all countries, the war years had meant the distortion
of economic development plans and time-tables. Perhaps in
India, where there was so much to be done and so little time
in which to do it, the effects of those years bore unusually
hard on the country. But the onset of peace certainly released
a massive dynamic drive which resulted in the attainment of
objectives which twenty years earlier would have seemed an
impracticable vision. The phrase 'the underdeveloped countries'
which has passed into the common currency of everyday
political and economic speech was new then, and I have the
impression that it was the Indian delegation to the first
Conference of the General Agreement on Tariffs and Trade in
1947 which first made it internationally known.

I recall the capacity and devotion of India's great men of
the time who shouldered burdens of staggering complexity
with imagination and determination. And in the welter of
their own problems I recall how they were courteously and
tolerantly ready to spare time to make my infinitely lesser
ones more manageable. In particular, nothing could exceed
the warm human kindliness of India's first President, Dr
Rajendra Prasad who had such a genius for inspiring affection
in all who had dealings with him. I am confident that the
place in history of this great man and beloved leader is
permanent and secure.

I was fortunate in having, at official levels, to deal with a
body of public servants who would have been in any country
and at any time a corps d'elite. That almost all of them
reached high office in India was only to be expected. They
deserved well—indeed richly—of their country. Many of them

must now be, like myself, in retirement: and I send them across the years and the continents my warmest personal greetings.

But my friends were by no means all official, and by no means either in the Central Government. My wife and I travelled widely in order to try to understand better India's vast, rich variety of resources, peoples, traditions and history. No one could have been more sympathetically received and more graciously helped by countless ordinary people throughout the country. To them I was a stranger whom they had never met before and in most cases were unlikely to meet again. But the warmth of personal relationships enabled my wife and myself to take away on our final departure imperishable recollections of innumerable acts of kindness and generosity. They were with her as long as she lived, and are with me today.

We were both especially happy in our relations with our Indian friends in Delhi in the Roshanara Club. To have been able, as the vice-president of the club, to greet the President of India on the great national occasions was an honour given, I should think, to few foreigners. I find most moving the recollection of the opportunity to serve my fellow members in this unusual way.

Although, in retrospect, recollections of personal relations are dominant, India's rich tapestry of resources provided other pictures on which to look back. No one with any historical sense could have failed to be stirred by the historical and architectural strata which were still to be detected and in imagination brought to life. Whether it is true to say that the present can only be understood by a knowledge of the past, it would be a dull person who would not react to what could be found in Delhi, which was my home twenty years ago. How appropriate it was that so many of the early annual Independence Day parades and processions laid colourful emphasis on India's history and traditions. My colour cine-films taken at the time preserve it all for me.

But one does not have to be a historical student to glow with pleasure at the sight and the thought of Delhi's magnificent natural setting—a city garlanded with flowering trees and the infinite variety of gardens with their kaleidoscope explosion of colour in the spring. I think I learned more about horticulture there than anywhere else and at any time. The few tropical or near-tropical plants which one can manage to grow in a modest country greenhouse in England are a spur to recollections of their counterparts growing in luxuriant profusion in their natural environment.

Does this answer the question as to what India means to me today? Very inadequately, I fear. One would have to be a Sarojini Naidu to find the right words. Let me borrow a few and say that I am proud and happy to have seen in my years in Delhi, India 'rise regenerate from thy gloom'; and to hear the future call 'with a manifold sound to crescent honours, splendours, victories vast.'

∼

ROWLAND OWEN was a bureaucrat who served as a senior British Trade Commissioner till 1952. He was also the vice-president of the Roshanara Club.

IV

Under the Indian Sun

~

STANLEY JEPSON

A former Editor of the Weekly *looks back. While in India he didn't become interested in yoga, but he could do the rope-trick!*

K.S.
21 February 1971

THIS IDEA IS FASCINATING and nostalgic. At seventy-six, and an insomniac, I feel like some old dame opening a precious jewel box in the night-watches. Inside are gems of happy memories. The most precious things one can collect perhaps, beyond diamonds or rubies. For I spent half my working life in India, some thirty years, first in the Indian Army and then for twenty years in a more comfortable (sometimes) editorial chair of this very paper! And I think I left my heart behind, for having lived in three continents I know now that in rural India are the most lovable of all peoples, deserving of all help and sympathy. So I planned to retire there and bought a nice house in that lovely, quiet hill-station, Matheran. But, alas, when I worked it out, I found the tax position would not allow that.

I got to India by accident, for in my teens I was a bound apprentice with a small weekly newspaper, first at the handsome pay of five shillings a week. Though my Pa was Managing Director, he thought I should learn from the bottom upwards, but nobody spent any time teaching me anything. In the second year I rose to seven shillings weekly; then I was in charge of a district on my pushbike at £2 per week which was then what I could pay my landlady.

In 1914, the First World War broke out and I made my dear mother weep by joining up with the 14th Mid. Regt., known as 'The Public Schools' Dn' though I never went to one—just winning a grammar school scholarship. The frustration of being office dogs-body was followed by the equal frustration of drilling with broomsticks and navvy work on trenches outside London. Next to me was the bright-eyed son of a general named Leggatt who discovered we could get three weeks leave if we applied to enter the Civil Service Army Entrance exam, which we did successfully, though the peppery old C.O. looked hard at Leggatt and muttered something about 'Your father put you up to this Army Regulation?' We sat for the exam after our leave and the first hundred were privileged to select Sandhurst or the new Military College in the then empty Staff College in Quetta. As the papers were full of tough-looking Gurkhas with kukris, we eventually found ourselves at Quetta, gentlemen cadets being tailored for the Indian Army.

IN A NEW WORLD

I was now in a new world, mounted on a horse with a sword which I didn't know how to use (Quetta never taught us that, though we made bridges, blew up trees, listened to long lectures, etc.). My regiment was the 40th Pathans, with many trans-frontier tribesmen like Orakzais, Afridis, etc., and as tough a crowd as you could imagine, reared in a land of blood-feuds. It was 1916 and many of our war wounded came back from France and I had to learn a little Pushtu to talk to them and deal with their pensions and affairs. Each month I rode to the old Fort at Fatehgarh on the Ganges to be paid just under Rs 400 in jingling rupees and the senior subaltern had 'arranged' that my bearer Chutton should take charge of my cash as I didn't know the prices or customs and 'It's better, old boy, to be done down by one man rather than a crowd, and he won't do you down.' He didn't, and served me faithfully until I left India and still writes me affectionate letters and I remember him each Christmas. Worth his weight in gold, but often, when I would tell him to put out some clothes in the evening so I could visit the club, he shook his head and remarked something about no more club till next month!

I knew a little Urdu, for we all had to pass this exam, and in our chummery mess when someone demanded a chhota peg I told him, 'Hamare waste bhi'... but that drink never came and I saw a reproving look in his eye. He had no intention of letting me waste money! One day he observed: 'We are going to buy a gun and do some shikar.' 'We' did, and had good times with other chaps.

A SALAAM FOR THE RAJ

One day, riding to the parade ground in the early morning, I was astonished when a little babu riding along dismounted, put down his brolly, salaamed and let me by, then remounted. I was speechless and, when I told fellow officers about this, they told me: 'He's the village postmaster, he was not salaaming you but the British Raj, his employer. Don't flatter yourself!' This was an old-time aspect of India which may amuse readers and sure astonished me.

India was then full of racial prejudice long since gone, happily. One evening I took to a club dance a pretty girl I had met and the club secretary drew me quietly aside and rebuked me, saying: 'Kindly don't invite her again, but let her stay for now.' She was slightly Anglo-Indian though it wasn't obvious, but he knew. This so upset me I didn't go to to the club for many weeks as a quiet protest.

In late 1916, I think it was, I found myself in the old German East Africa, now Tanzania, chasing Von Lettow, the great German soldier, in dense bush which my fellow soldiers, the hillmen from (NWFP), hated like hell. We captured Dar es Salaam, and moved along the longest line of communication in history south to Kilwa and Lindi and towards Central Africa. I found a new respect for the Pathans (then mostly Yusufzais), gallant Dogras and tough Punjabi Muslims, especially during the Id when they kept the fast in a hot climate during the day. I got bad malaria and other diseases, but measles saved my life once.

Our Medical Officer, Col. Haji, MC, drew me outside Colonel our tent one day and looked at my spots. 'Prickly heat,' I observed. 'Open your month, Jeppo, please,' and he diagnosed measles and left me behind in a tent in quarantine for a fortnight. I was astonished as I'd had measles as a kid. 'We cannot have this spreading when we are moving off tomorrow,' said Haji. The man who took over my company was shot through the head and the other company officer died from bad burns when the Germans set fire to the dry grass. I joined up later, very sorrowful!

Under the Indian Sun Again

Back in India I tried to settle down, made up my mind I was not cut out for soldiering and resigned. I was a regular and could do this with a three-year pension, owing to the glut of young captains. Returning home I tried my hand as a freelance journalist, then back to my old weekly's office as assistant editor, got fed up again, and joined the *Yorkshire Post*, and after two years pined for the Indian sun and the silken east! I applied for two jobs and got offers from the *Statesman* and from the *Times of India*. I was interviewed by Sir Stanley Reed, in London. God rest his soul—he lived to be over ninety. The Calcutta offer was much better than the Bombay one, so I offered to take the 'T of I' job on condition I was sold a block of shares. After looking at me with a peculiar glint, Sir Stanley agreed, and I went to Bombay to take charge of the *Times of India Weekly*, as it was then called.

I found we had more readers than any other paper in India, an inspiring thought; for by reason of distance and distribution in the night the four main dailies then were restricted to areas around Bombay, Madras, Calcutta and Lahore. We then sold at 6 annas, and it was assumed that families would pass on the paper, instead of using it for wrapping up as with a newspaper, so we could multiply our circulation by three or four or more.

Indian Ladies Swim in Public

I liked and enjoyed this work and made many friends, mostly Indian. With a domestic staff of bygone days we were able, in our Marine Lines flat, to entertain people who wrote for my paper, and they were predominantly Indian. I joined clubs, not the Royal Yacht, as I disliked their rule excluding Indians in India, but I liked the Willingdon, and recall the days when it was proposed to build a swimming bath, and raised eyebrows when committee men suggested that 'Indian ladies might not like to swim in public!' La la, how they liked it and how well they did it! How old-fashioned can some folks get! I also joined the Cricket Club of India, as it was near my flat and I could swim there before hazri, which I liked. But I thought the membership rather too large for cosiness.

I was fortunate in having a fine editor's secretary, R.V. Iyer, who still writes to me from Delhi. He saved me a lot of work because we devised stock letters for stock enquiries. For instance if we had some very pretty Indian girl on the cover, some old gentleman would write in to say he wished to write to her on one excuse or another, and requested her name and address. This we never did, of course, but I'd say, 'You know the answer to that, R.V. ... letter D.' This said the photograph was a very old one, that we had no present address and probably by now the lady might well be a grandmother! No more trouble with him.

When I resigned from the army, I got myself a bride, still with me, not her old self now though, owing to a stroke. She thought up the idea of getting together child readers in a Young Folks' League, and inviting their letters. Oh, the hundreds of letters that came in with all kinds of problems and a few lines in reply to each. When she went sick I once undertook the job of reading and replying in brief lines ... it was a full-time job. Midnight oil all right! We got these kids together in Bombay with outings to Juhu, etc., and happy times we had with a banner with 'Weekly Y.F.L.' flying.

The idea was that Brown, White, Pink or Ginger should get together and learn racial harmony ere the adults poisoned their little minds with racialism. I think it worked. I saw them on the beach. They wore badges designed by Aunty Gwen (my wife), with various colours—black, brown, blue, grey—their eyes we told them. Also I think this was a circulation-building programme, with our numbered copies giving birth dates with small prizes ... not to mention our crosswords, but that was not my department.

MONKEYS DON'T FEAR SNAKES

Any editor must get away and relax, and when I saw that, with the Second World War going on and on (self in charge of A.R.P. Controls), it was unlikely I could take home leave for many years, I sought and bought a retreat in Matheran, built by the railway line and called Aman Lodge. A kind Parsi friend let us have this for a very reasonable sum. We spent many happy weekends there and became part-time farmers, sinking a well and growing all sorts of things from large pineapples, bananas, guavas, etc. Sacred monkeys were our headache. One man said they feared snakes, so our cementwallah made cement painted snakes; but we found monkeys sitting on them eating our fruit. Nets I bought proved useless for they were up and over in no time. We were not allowed to shoot them, though one genius said a charge of salt instead of lead would wound and not kill, but I didn't like this idea. Their babies hung around their tummies. The brightest idea was cut-up flypapers stuck on tomatoes and lettuces, etc., which got on their fingers. But they still defeated us. Friends said the jungle would reclaim it and this would be known in future as 'Jepson's Folly'. Oh no, it is now a park.

TAXES WERE HIGH EVEN THEN

This bungalow had its own railway station as it had been built by a man who built the line from Neral Junction. This was a great convenience and enabled us to take up items like a pump for the well we sank with Thakur labour, while I had to do the plumbing! But in the end we got what the water-diviner, old Cassini, promised: 3000 gallons minimum in dry season and limitless in autumn. So we had a big tank and water aqueducts for our plot, now owned by the municipality. I had hoped to retire there, but, alas, found the Indian taxation prevented this, so came to an island where the taxation fitted my income. Those were happy relaxing week-ends and I often wonder what became of all the schemes for rope railways and other developments for this little paradise in the hills, only 3,000 feet high but quiet and fresh. No cars! [*The position even today remains just the same.*—Ed.]

Another way I relaxed was by going into the high forests of the then Central Provinces, East and West Khandesh. My old regimental colonel had taught me shikar and I often made long trips when leave permitted. Had some exciting and tense moments also. Other writers sent me their excitements and we published 'Tense Moments with Big Game' and later I got an edited book out of this subject. Friends in the Willingdon often pulled my leg when I ran a campaign for preservation of wildlife in India. But I was then, and am still, convinced that it is not the sportsman who diminishes game but the poacher who sells venison and horns and hides—I've seen these piled up in a Bombay deep-freeze. The sportsman removes only the old males, which is biologically good for the herd. But in the end I grew so fond of wildlife, I did not shoot anything except cattle-lifting leopards or tigers and the brutal crocodiles.

The War in Pictures

Our firm took on the wartime job of countering German propaganda magazines, the idea being to persuade India that the Allies had resources to ensure victory. Our rotogravure press was considered suitable and I was asked to edit this also. 'The man from the ministry' had a talk on languages in India (before Partition that was)—I thought with dialects over 100 or more. But I suggested we could start with six or seven and then expand, say, Urdu, Hindi, Punjabi, Bengali, Gurkhali, Tamil, Kannada, etc. The idea was to use the same pictures of the war effort and replace the captions in various languages. I told him I did not think the villagers could all read. That didn't matter ... the copies would be given away and the headman would explain and he could read.

My team of translators had some pretty problems. 'How do I translate depth charge ... blitzkrieg ... Hurricane fighter, etc., etc?' Imagining what strange words I'd get in various lingos I advised them all to keep to the original and play safe! The magazine poured off our press day and night and only with much manoeuvring could I get my own paper printed!

A Vertical Problem

Then the man from the ministry said he'd like a Chinese

edition to fly over the 'hump', when Japan was preparing for its offensive against India. 'But Chinese is read top to bottom and our captions are horizontal,' I expostulated. Not to worry, the folks would look at the photograph and then turn the paper sideways! I asked how they were distributing it into remote villages, and was told by bullock-carts which carried soap and kerosene. All part of the war effort and not my problem!

When the war against Japan was over, I pleaded with the powers in Delhi to keep this magazine running for village uplift, better hygiene, irrigation, prenatal care and dozens of other items needed in India. Alas, they had no money for this, even though we produced a dummy magazine for four annas with a view to attracting good advertising. I still think they missed a fine chance. For India needs some such guidance in her many heart-rending problems, some common ideals to unify and give faith and hope to the millions of toiling villagers in conditions which would break the heart of any Western farmer. They must be the toughest and most deserving peasantry on earth.

THE ROPE-TRICK

Another of my hobbies was home-cine and I started the Amateur Cine Society of India which still flourishes. I shudder now to think what I spent on this hobby, but this brings me to the final joke.

Every newspaper editor knows what the 'silly season' means or used to. It was a flat period when good news did not break and one had to provide something. So our beloved managing director, 'E.G.P.', said to me one day: 'Jepson, any ideas for the silly season?' I told him I had one, and that a man called Ibn Batuta had perpetuated the myth of the Indian Rope-Trick and I suggested we should offer a goodly sum for anyone who could do this in the open air without any theatre props, etc. I think we fixed on something like Rs 50,000. Anyway, the offer remained open a long time and, though lots of folks knew someone else who had seen it, nobody came forward to claim this handsome reward, which confirmed my suspicion that it was a myth based on mass hypnotism!

Then I made a film of this trick. You can do anything on film, of course. The sadhu could not climb the rope as he was too heavy and it was a trick rope—hose-pipe with rope outside and a steel rod inside. The boy climbed all right and bits of his body came down to earth—an old doll painted brown and dismembered and thrown down. The crowd reaction shots were taken when my friend the sadhu (an employee at the Colaba docks) did conjuring tricks and I stood on a box and shot the faces.

When the film was ready, I invited our managing director and his wife to dinner and suggested here was the rope-trick in the open air and what about the Rs 50,000? He laughed at this and said I was not eligible as a staff member, which was what I had expected. But I did win a gold medal in London for the film with the Institute of Amateur Cine.

What happy days and happy memories! My hope for India is that she can solve her problems in the spirit of faith and racial harmony. She reminds me through her various tribulations of a great elephant shrugging off whatever elephants do shrug off.

I often listen to the Indian National Anthem on a record and bow my head humbly, for India has taught me so much.

~

STANLEY JEPSON was editor of *The Illustrated Weekly of India* and spent thirty years in India, the first ten years in the Indian army and the rest as a journalist and editor.

V

At Home in India

~

SIR ARTHUR DEAN

IT STARTED CASUALLY, just a job; and soon it meant engrossment in the work, a home, friends; India became a way of life.

First and foremost it meant a job. After the Armistice at the end of 1918, I saw an Army order which said assistant engineers were wanted in the Indian Public Works Department. I applied for one of these posts. I was interviewed in London and also had a medical examination after which I was given an appointment and sailed for India. I reported in Bombay and was sent up to Nagpur, having been put on the cadre of the Central Provinces and Berar of which Nagpur was the capital. I was very shortly posted to the office of the Executive Engineer, Amraoti, Berar, for training. Fairly soon I was put in charge of a sub-division and found the work very interesting.

I did all my journeys on a bicycle, getting along the roads and the banks of the canals. This way, I put in quite a lot of inspection as one was always ready to stop.

I learnt a good deal of the practical side of engineering from the Indian overseers. They helped me a great deal also in learning the language, which I found difficult. I never reached a particularly high standard but was quite fluent. The technically trained Indian officers at all levels spoke and wrote

English almost as well as I did myself. It was from them that I learnt all I ever knew, not only about Indian design and construction methods, but also the educational system at all levels up to Technical College and University.

A New Home

India also meant a home for me. I had got married in January 1916 during short leave from France and our first child, John, was born in 1917. So when I was given the job as an Assistant Engineer, Public Works Department, Central Provinces, India, and went there in September 1919, my wife and son joined me.

We settled down as a family, which grew with the addition of three more children, and made ourselves comfortably at home in the various places—Yeotmal, Akola, Jubbulpore, Indore and Delhi—to which I was posted.

India also meant a career for me. This was a career of considerable engineering and administrative interest. I progressed from 1919 to 1946 through various stages of Assistant, Executive, Superintending and Chief Engineer responsible for the design and construction of many works of considerable technical novelty and complexity. One of these was a road bridge over the Narmada river on the Nagpur-Jubbulpore road, designed as a matter of economy to be over-topped by high floods. I wrote a technical paper about this published by the Institution of Civil Engineers for which I was awarded the Coopers Hill medal. Another interesting project was the public-works side of the anti-malaria scheme designed by Sir Gordon Covell, the malariologist, to control malaria in the Delhi Union area.

CIVIL AVIATION

I was the first Superintending Engineer for civil aviation in India and dealt with the all-up air-route to Australia in the section from the Persian Gulf to Malaya. This was initially for Flying Boats requiring landing sites on water. One such was at the confluence of the Jumna and Ganges rivers near Allahabad. When land planes took over, runways had to be built and also various technical installations for direction finding and so on. Also, large hangars in which the planes could be serviced and repaired as required. At Karachi, the hangars were designed and constructed of pre-stressed reinforced concrete. Ultimately I became the Chief Engineer of the Central Public Works Department which was in charge of all central government works throughout India.

On completion of five years as Chief Engineer, I was asked to take over as Chairman of the Delhi Improvement Trust. I was given a five-year term for continuing work for the improvement of conditions in the over-crowded old city, removing slums and building new quarters, improving sewerage and sewer disposal and increasing piped water supply. This post came under the ministry of health. While in the Central Public Works Department, my minister was Dr Ambedkar. I found him competent and anxious to improve conditions for the poorest of the people, but not easily approachable. In the Delhi Improvement Trust, my minister was the only woman in Pandit Nehru's cabinet, Raj Kumari Kaur. She was competent and very charming and occasionally saw me directly to get things moving.

Last, but not least, India meant to me a very friendly relationship with a number of interesting and pleasant people.

When I went as executive engineer to Jubbulpore, the Superintending Engineer was an Indian officer, Rai Bahadur Sunderlal, who was a very good and friendly man. Not long after, Dewan Bahadar B.C. Dube became chief Engineer. He also was a very friendly person, and a good administrator.

About this time, I went to Indore. I met a number of maharajas among whom His Highness of Rutlam and His Highness of Alwar stood out in my memory as very friendly people. The latter had a school of artists in the traditional Rajput style, working in his state and I still have in my drawing-room a painting from this school that he gave me.

While in Indore, I was offered a vacancy in the Central Public Works Department with headquarters in Delhi. Mr Hyde, CIE, MC, was then Chief Engineer, Central Provinces, and he facilitated the transfer. In Delhi I met a number of Indian officers, all of whom I found efficient and warm-hearted. In my early service in India I heard of some clubs which refused to admit Indian members. I never joined a club that did this.

Khan Bahadur Mohammed Suleiman was a great friend of mine. When, in the winter of 1963–64, my wife and I visited India and Pakistan to see old friends, Mohammed Suleiman was on the quay at Karachi to greet us, and later entertained us in Lahore. In New Delhi we were put up by Sir Sobha Singh and Lady Sobha Singh and they have since visited us at our home in England. During our trip to India, Noor Mohammed, who was my driver for twenty-six years, met us on the station at Jubbulpore, together with Ram Din who had worked for us from 1919 to 1948 and to whom I give a small pension of Rs 30 a month. In Pakistan we met Akbar Hayat Khan Noon, an engineer who had been recruited to the Central

Public Works Department when I was Chief Engineer.

India means to me a friendship of lasting value with the sub-continent.

~

Sir Arthur William Henry Dean joined as Assistant Engineer in the Indian Public Works Department in 1918. He had a distinguished career, finally becoming Chief Engineer and also Chairman of Delhi Improvement Trust. He died in 1976.

VI

Bitten by the Indian Bug

~

HORACE ALEXANDER

THE REAL INDIA is the humble men and women who heroically give their lives to lessen the sorrows of the poorest, the most oppressed, the most needy.

I grew up in a household that was worldwide in outlook. My father had travelled to China, and his Chinese friends visited us in our English home. He had many French friends, so the French language was often heard in our home. He had also visited India with the British government's Opium Commission of 1894 (as a member of the Opposition, so to speak).

Two Indian students were my contemporaries at King's: L.K. Hyder, whom I knew slightly and liked, and who rediscovered me forty years later one day in Delhi. He was then, and had for long been, on the staff of Aligarh College, and he was, I found a nationalist Muslim, not a follower of Mr Jinnah. The other was Rama Rao, destined for a distinguished career in India; he lived for a time on the same staircase, but we only had the most casual acquaintance.

Some ten years later, perhaps in 1924, I was asked by a friend in Birmingham, where I was teaching, whether I would be willing to meet a man called C.F.Andrews. I had never heard of him, but he came to call, and unexpectedly he changed the course of my life.

At that time Andrews was battling against the Indian government's excise policy. The League of Nations was trying to curb the world drug trade, and there was soon to be a conference in Geneva, when all the countries that grew opium or were otherwise involved with the traffic would have to explain their policies. Andrews wanted to find someone in England who would keep in touch with his effort in India and help to challenge the official policy he expected the Indian government to present at Geneva.

THE FIRST SIGHT

His friend and mine, Jack Hoyland, who had spent some years teaching at Hislop Christian College at Nagpur, sent him to me because my father had spent a good part of his life challenging the British policy of selling opium to China. With some reluctance I agreed to try to help, assuming that it would be a short-term assignment. However, a year or two later, I was due for a sabbatical leave from my job of teaching international relations.

So far, 'international relations' had been to me mainly European affairs; but anyone could see that problems of Empire, of the relations of Europe to Asia and Africa, were soon going to be of great importance. So perhaps I could learn something at first hand by visiting India and some other Asian countries that were under European rule. If, at the same time, I made an independent study of drug addiction in its several forms in India, Malaya, Java and perhaps elsewhere, it would give me a solid reason for going about these countries; and I might learn a lot of other things as I travelled. I think this happened. The drug enquiry was a very convenient starting point for meeting all kinds of people: government officials, missionaries, social workers, Indian politicians, and many more—even some of the 'addicts'.

Some unexpected things happened to me. I went to India with the conviction that the English were just, fair-minded people genuinely concerned about preparing India to follow the footsteps of Canada and Australia into true and effective self-government. Although I had heard mostly favourable reports of Gandhi, I did not understand why he was so determined to organize campaigns of civil disobedience. Of course, I saw much that I could admire in the work of the British in India, but I learnt some things that I found very disturbing.

THE REALITY

Looking back at the whole experience afterwards, I found myself singling out an experience I had in Orissa. My host there, an Englishman, whom I had known slightly at Cambridge, happened also to be a fellow Quaker. As we sat at breakfast, his *mali* came in sight working in the garden outside the window. He looked as if he had never had a square meal in his life. 'Do you really think,' said my host, 'that a man like that gardener is ready for democratic self-government?' The mentality behind this remark seemed to me so appalling that I found myself wondering what could have happened to a decent-minded young man to enable him, after twenty years, to develop such a jaundiced mind.

Later the same day, a British official came to see me, to talk about opium addiction in that area, which was high; for this part of Orissa was one of the 'black spots' of opium consumption, where a special government enquiry was at the moment going on. After we had talked for a time, suddenly the British official (he was Irish, I believe) broke off and began walking up and down the room as he passionately declaimed, 'Why does a man like you come all this distance and travel round the country enquiring about opium? Can't you see the things that really matter here? It is not opium that matters. It is the way these unhappy people are governed, or rather, grossly misgoverned. Why don't you stop your drug enquiry and concentrate on that?'

I had, indeed, already seen things and felt even more, that made me very open to this accusation. At that very time there had been a serious flood in Orissa but, as far as I could see, the official line was to try to minimize it, and to insist that there had been few casualties and that no special relief funds were needed. This kind of thing did not fit my idea of the British shouldering the 'white man's burden'. I began to think that the sooner India took charge of her own affairs, the better—not so much that things would necessarily be much better for the poor Indians; but they would be much better for the arrogant British—or so I hoped.

AND THE MAHATMA

A few days before I left India I spent a week with Mahatma Gandhi in his ashram at Sabarmati. There was something about that place that made an immediate appeal to me. Apart from Gandhi himself, I made friends with his remarkable secretary, Mahadev Desai; I also came to know Miraben (Madeleine Slade) who had been there, I think, less than a year. From that time on, I was very ready to support C.F. Andrews in matters of much wider significance than the official drug policy. (Actually, my own conclusions in that matter, as also I think the attitude of Mahatma Gandhi himself, was less completely hostile to the official position than I had expected it to be: for in India at that time there really was a good deal of harmless drug taking, that could not be called addiction, but was truly described as 'semi-medicinal'. But the official slogan: 'Maximum revenue with minimum consumption' seemed to me very dubious to say the least.)

I did not really expect ever to visit India again. But the 'bug' had somehow got into me. I began to correspond with Gandhi and with other friends at Santiniketan and elsewhere. Amiya Chakravarty, one of Tagore's finest young Santiniketan teachers, was invited to our Quaker college, Woodbrooke, Birmingham, for a year. The friendship with Charlie Andrews grew closer all the time. He sent me to India to try to negotiate an understanding between Lord Irwin and Mr Gandhi in 1930; and what I saw of both those men at that time made me very ready for the Gandhi–Irwin Pact a few months later. Then came Mr Gandhi's visit to London for the Round Table Conference, when I gave a day or two each week trying to make myself useful, and so became ever more closely identified with Mr Gandhi personally and with his demand for Indian freedom. So I came to know Pyarelal and Devdas Gandhi.

A group called the India Conciliation Group came into being, largely inspired by the single-minded devotion of a remarkable woman, Agatha Harrison.

BACK AGAIN

A new chapter came into my life and the connection with India when, in 1942, very soon after the death of my wife who had been an invalid for many years, the Friends Ambulance Unit in London asked me to accompany a small section who were going to Calcutta on the invitation of the government to assist in civil defence measures, which seemed essential with the Japanese rapidly advancing through Burma.

The year I spent in Calcutta was an unusual experience. As our group of young English men and women had come under government auspices, it was no doubt useful in the first place for them to have me to help in building confidence on the unofficial side. Indeed, Richard Symonds and I, who were the advance party, visited Mr Gandhi at Sevagram before we even went to Delhi. Mahadev Desai gave us a write-up in *Harijan*. We persuaded a young Indian, whom I had known as a student in England, Sudhir Ghosh, to live with us in Calcutta; and week by week we invited Indian leaders, including Dr Shyama Prasad Mukherji, Shaheed Suhrawardy and his brother, and various other members of the Congress, Muslim League and others, to spend evenings with us.

They all came, and seemed to enjoy the company of a group of young English people, who had no official position to uphold. But after the 'Quit India' movement was launched, and the Congress leaders were mostly in jail, my presence was probably an embarrassment to the Unit. I returned to England in the summer of 1943, but by that time two things had happened which had long-term effects.

First, the October 1942 cyclone hit the Midnapore district, and gave us a much bigger job to tackle than anything connected

with Japanese bombing. There followed the Bengal famine of
1943 and my job on my return to England was to help in
securing funds for relief of the famine—not an easy undertaking
in the midst of the war; but people in England showed an
amazing generosity. Then, too, I made friends with Mr
Rajagopalachari, the only top Congress leader who was not
in jail.

I was back again in India in January 1946, this time with
the full support of the new Secretary of State, Lord Pethick-
Lawrence, who was trying to build bridges to the Congress
leaders. My time was divided between relief activities, mainly
in Bengal and meetings with Mr Gandhi and some of his
associates. I had known Jawaharlal Nehru at a much earlier
date; but it was only now that our acquaintance developed
into friendship. Anyone who was closely associated with Mr
Gandhi inevitably came to know most of the other Congress
leaders quite intimately. This included Sardar Patel, who became
Sudhir Ghosh's supporter during the months of negotiation
leading to the final withdrawal of the British. On the other
side, the work of the India Conciliation Group had brought
me into personal touch with Sir Stafford Cripps; so when the
Cabinet Mission came to India, I found myself in close contact
with both sides.

I was with Mr Gandhi for a few days during his heroic
walks through Bengal in the early months of 1947; and I was
again with him and Shaheed Suhrawardy for the fateful days
of Independence when their extraordinary partnership helped
to bring sudden peace to the great city of Calcutta, after a
year of almost constant communal clashes. And I was with
him again in Delhi a few days before his death.

I stayed on in India for some years after the coming of Independence, and in those early years I was also able to pay several visits to Pakistan, where I made friends with several of the leaders. But it seemed that nothing any of us could do, quietly behind the scenes, any more than the effort of various UN official commissions, could heal the breach caused by the conflict over Kashmir.

It is idle, perhaps, to try and disentangle the whole tangled web of conflicting attitudes and actions that have made this one of the most intractable disputes of our time. I recall one conversation from the early days, with the American journalist Louis Fischer. I suggested that it would be a good idea to try to find what the people of Kashmir really wanted, and if it was independence from both countries, could not that be accepted? 'Oh, no,' said Fischer. 'You must not talk like that. Whoever would care to know what the people want ! It is only power that counts in this world.'

Through Teething Pains

Professor Suhrawardy once said to me: 'You seem to be concerned to help people who are suffering from catastrophes. So I think you will need to stay in India for quite a long time.' Fortunately, there has not been anything comparable to the disasters of the Bengal famine and the aftermath of Partition in the Punjab in recent years, until the terrible East Pakistan cyclone of 1970. But it would not be difficult to find a place of special need each year. However, my own stay in free India did not last more than some eight or ten years. I stayed long enough to see the start of Vinoba Bhave's Bhoodan work; to see the first Five-Year Plan launched; to see the new Constitution in operation; to see a democratic system of government operating, on a basis of adult suffrage; not working as well as some had hoped, but at least working.

What is the picture that seems to emerge after these twenty-five years of self-government? First, India has had an impressive succession of able leaders, men of integrity (women too), who compare well with the leaders of any country in the world. But the political leadership at the local level is not so impressive.

WHAT REMAINS TO BE DONE

Certainly, there has been progress of a kind, but acute poverty has not been overcome. Land has not been generally distributed. Unemployment has not been abolished. Even the taint of untouchability is evidently by no means abolished in the villages. Such changes of ancient social abuses are bound to be slow, no doubt. To the outward eye, it would seem that the changes that Gandhi and his colleagues hoped to achieve are slow to arrive. Perhaps the mistake, partly, is to expect too much from government action.

The most fundamental question is: What is happening in the realm of pioneering effort? Is the sense of social responsibility on the increase? It has always been difficult to generalize about such a vast and varied country as India. One must try to look below the surface. Month by month I look at the Planning Commission periodical *Yojana*, which often has a page devoted to the efforts of some obscure man or woman, or sometimes a group, who are pioneering some new enterprise, up and down the country. No one can know how many such hidden efforts there are in the whole land; but even if there are only a few, it is such efforts that keep a land healthy and give it hope—not the manoeuvring of the political leaders. And the Ṣarvodaya movement, started by Gandhi, is not dead. Opinions may differ as to the actual achievements of the work started by Vinoba Bhave; but it is certain that a number of his fellow workers are giving their lives to the needs of the poorest. It may well be true, as Indira Gandhi was reported as saying recently, that if Gandhi were alive today he would have much the same criticisms to make as he had when he was alive. But I think he would also acknowledge that there are, spread around India, numbers of heroic men and women, giving themselves, without thought of self, to the care of the needy. Their deeds are never reported in the press, and probably never will be; but they are the real builders of a new India, working from the foundations laid by the wise men of old.

~

HORACE ALEXANDER was an English Quaker teacher and writer, pacifist and ornithologist. He joined Sidney Dillon Ripley on an expedition to the Naga hills in 1950 and also associated himself with a group of birdwatchers in New Delhi. He died in 1989.

VII

My Discovery of India

~

TAYA ZINKIN

IN THE DAYS when human values prevailed and power did not isolate leaders from the masses, the discovery of India had its own rewards—and a foreigner could look upon the people and the country as part of 'an extended family'.

When I glibly agreed to write for this series, I did not realize what I was letting myself in for. For me India means so much, and at so many levels, that it is almost impossible for me to order the thoughts and bring into play the discipline which many years of journalism should have drummed into me.

For me India has been all at once a leap into the unknown—adventure, romance, self-realization, the chance to grow up, the opportunity to fulfil myself. India gave me my home, my family, my career and many of my friends. I spent the best years of my life in India and, whatever reputation I have enjoyed as a journalist, I owe it to India.

Before the Second World War, when I was studying medicine in Paris, I was completely ignorant of India. I was so ignorant that the first time I heard the name of Gandhi was when my friend Grisha, dressed in a sheet and adorned by an alarm clock, turned up as the Mahatma at a fancy dress dance on the Riviera.

FANCY BELIEFS

Having had, at school, to memorize the names of Pondicherry, Chandernagore, Karaikal, Yanaon and Mahe, I thought that most of India was French. That some, probably small and unimportant, part of India was British dawned upon me in 1938 when Maurice Zinkin, a young man I had run into at Cambridge, left for Bombay to serve in what must have been the British equivalent of the French colonial administration.

Like so many of my compatriots I used to believe that the richest and most important of all the maharajas was Kapurthala. Tales of his parties, which were fabulously wild, were doing the rounds in Paris, including the account of a dance at which he distributed precious stones to those of his guests daring enough to pluck them from the collars of ferocious watch-dogs.

Finally, in a very hazy way, India was Rudyard Kipling's Kim, the heroic Hurree Chunder Mookerji, the saintly Lama, the wry Mahbub Ali, the garrulous hill ranee, the colourful Grand Trunk Road.

Not until I married Maurice Zinkin and went to India at the end of the Second World War did I discover that most of India was British, that Kapurthala was a minor prince and that the characters of *Kim*, including the Grand Trunk Road, were eternal.

As I settled down to becoming an unorthodox sari-wearing ICS (Indian Civil Service) wife, I fell in love with India. I sided with the Congress against perfidious Albion, a thing which came easily to me, since I had never forgiven them for

Joan of Arc. Falling in love with India and siding against the British require no explanation; siding with the Congress, however, does.

I had always been against colonialism, whether it is called imperialism or simply colonialism, not because of the exploitation it pre-supposes, but because people ought to be allowed to run their own lives and make their own mistakes. Whether India would be better run by Indian politicians than by the ICS under a Viceroy was for Indians themselves to decide. In any case I was not very impressed by the British record in India: there were not enough hospitals, not enough schools or roads.

The social inequalities were shocking. Indians, far more than Britons, were guilty of waste, glaring conspicuous consumption. Indeed, many of them had to be truly heartless to behave the way they did. I still remember the thirteen-row and 3000-carat emerald necklace one Indian businessman used to wear on grand occasions. Besides this he had a pearl necklace which he boasted was insured for one million pounds and which he had had great difficulty in preserving from Lady Willingdon's admiration. This same gentleman, who did not seem moved by the sight of beggars and pot-bellied children, used to employ cooks to feed the crows of his native town. The crows were fed such excellent food that I asked to be given the same fare rather than eat the tasteless 'Angrezi' vegetarian meals they had been told to prepare for me.

WEALTH AND POVERTY

A day at the Bombay races used to be a spectacle, a peep into a fairytale come true: in the most exclusive enclosure, Indians, bedecked like Christmas trees, used to glitter with jewels. Those were the days when, to go to the races, ladies wore the sort of fineries one now sees only at a performance on a dancer. This display of wealth was in brazen contrast to the surrounding poverty. Until I arrived in India I used to believe that I knew what poverty looked like. I had seen Spain and Poland, I had seen the West Indies and North Africa and I had first-hand knowledge of Harlem and New York's slums. In Paris I had worked with destitutes. But nowhere had I seen anything approaching the poverty of India. Somehow I did not blame that poverty on the British. But I felt that so long as the British remained in India as an imperial power, the more glaring inequalities would remain because there are some things which people can only do for themselves, whether it is abolishing untouchability or bringing about a modicum of social justice and personal shame.

Until I arrived in India in 1945, I had taken no interest in politics whatsoever; indeed I had never read the newspapers, with the exception of the *Canard Enchaine*. During the war I had followed the news on the air. But to be in India at the end of 1945 and not to become involved in Indian politics was impossible. The question which was agitating everybody was: 'Would India be able to rule itself?' Having met Nehru, Patel and Rajaji—to mention only a few of the senior politicians— I had no doubt that, with the help of the extremely able Indian members of the ICS, they would manage very well.

As I became increasingly involved and interested in India's future, I took every opportunity to travel and meet as many people, from as many spheres, as possible, besides my husband's service colleagues and their wives who received me, as one of them, with open arms.

On the boat, coming out to rejoin Maurice, I had learnt quite a lot of Hindustani, unfortunately from a very charming British officer who had an atrociously *koi hai* accent, which I never quite managed to shed. This was particularly infuriating since French and Hindi or Urdu have a great many sounds in common and I would have had no foreign accent had I learnt from an Indian. However, by the time I landed in Bombay I could speak enough pidgin, something to get on by myself with those who did not speak English. No sooner did I get to Delhi than I began to learn Urdu, and later Hindi. This was most helpful for I travelled extensively, often in second class by train, and I was able to engage in limited but useful conversation. In Delhi too, particularly in Old Delhi where I frequently cycled on some treasure hunt to Chor Bazar, I made it a point to chat with all those ready to listen to my improvised attempts to stretch the limits of my vocabulary. Long before All India Radio tried and failed to get its message over I resorted to circumlocutions such as '*mujhe is chiz baitne ki upper mirbanise dena*' which invariably produced a *mora* or a chair in the little Chandni Chowk shops.

RESPECT FOR AUTHORITY

The more I travelled about and the more I met people from all walks of life, the more I became convinced that India was, and would be, easy to govern. In those days Indians had a habit of looking to authority with respect; they felt that the 'Ma Bap Sarkar' had their interest at heart, and so were remarkably law-abiding. Such unquestioned faith in the government put a heavy burden of noblesse oblige upon the rulers. With very few exceptions, the ICS officers I met before and after

Independence did live up to the people's expectations. This, however, did not always hold true for the politicians who did not hesitate to use the masses like pawns in the power game. If India has become difficult to govern, it is the fault of the Indian politicians.

Pre-Independence India was steeped in an unreal atmosphere, perhaps because the leaders had been playing the political game without realizing that the independence of which they talked so much was so close at hand. When it came they were not ready for it—Jinnah excepted. Sarojini Naidu was perhaps the most typical of that Alice in Wonderland mood. She used to hold court in Sir Sri Ram's mansion where she lived in great style, surrounded by adoration, bantering with devastating wit like Dorothy Parker, ordering people about with matronly aplomb, running international conferences, driving her doctors mad, devouring the candle of life from both ends. Despite her strict diet she would insist on coming to dinner only if there was going to be roast duck and sparkling company; the champagne was provided, as always, by that scintillating raconteur, Sardar Panikkar, the panache by Colonel Lakshmi, the contemporary Rani of Jhansi, the intrigue by Sir C.P. Ramaswamy Aiyar.

FIRST ASSIGNMENT

In those days Pandit Nehru looked so young that, until the horrors of Partition hacked his real age into his face, I used to think he belonged to my own generation—until I met his daughter whose sons exactly sandwiched ours. Nehru lived at No. 17 York Road, across the road from us; he was already then Interim Prime Minister of India. I do not think he can have known who I was beyond being vaguely aware that he often saw me in his house, with his daughter. But his manners were so exquisite that whenever he passed me in his car, and I was on foot, he would tell his driver to stop and offer me a lift.

Indeed, it is because of those lifts and our occasional chats in his car because of my friendship with Indira, that I began to write. After Partition we went to England for a while. One evening, Donald McLachlan, the foreign editor of the *Economist* for whom Maurice had been writing something on the economic aspects of Independence, came to dinner. When I described Nehru he asked me to write a pen portrait of India's first prime minister. Thus began my journalistic career. Until my article was published in it, I had never read the *Economist*. While we were in England, I contributed another couple of articles on India and Pakistan for Donald and when Maurice went back to India, this time for a business firm, Donald asked me to be his correspondent for the subcontinent. I was a scientist by training, but the opportunity thus offered to continue to be in the thick of things, as in the days when Maurice had been in the government, was irresistible. I decided to give journalism a try.

Soon the *Guardian*, then of Manchester, asked me to become its correspondent, and so did *Le Monde*. The going was tough. For a decade, I travelled half the year going sometimes to places so remote that time had stood still for the local inhabitants. Thus as late as 1959, I was telling tribals that India had been independent since 1947 and it once fell to me, in Telengana, to break the terrible news of Lenin's death to a young activist. I travelled to Nepal in winter and walked down most of the way since the Indian road was only barely begun. I stayed with tree-dwellers in Kerala, and watched Ananda's rural complex grow in Kaira, Gujarat. One little plant pasteurizing milk near the station, a left-over from the war, was the seed for Amul, and a university was dreamt up under my eyes in the shade of a few trees. I saw India start the Bhakra Dam, the DVC, the Tungabhadra and the three steel complexes.

DISCOVERY OF INDIA

I watched India grow. The sight was exhilarating and I did my best to take my readers along with me in my unending discovery of India. With them I lived in remote villages watching the first experiments in community development as dreamt up by Albert Mayer, with them I stayed in the blue hills of Orissa watching the birth of Gramdan, with them I stayed in the waste that was going to become Chandigarh, even before Jane Drew and Maxwell Fry and Le Corbusier pitched their huts there. Above all, I tried to make my readers stay in those quiet villages where tradition is so strong that even the local medical officers went to the Snake Temple if bitten by a cobra; the villages where beauty is dispensed by the fingertips of the women adorning their huts to attract Goddess Lakshmi.

As I got to know India better I became convinced that there were two Indias: the India of the villages where even the electrical revolution is not destroying the dignity of life and the India which the outsiders know, the India of the metropolis, the slums and the politicians. I watched Nehru who had been so accessible even after his country became independent, become increasingly isolated, until one day in Amritsar, an old man who only wanted to touch his feet and receive *darshan* was nearly killed by a lathi and was carried away by the police in mufti. I watched the slow erosion power works on those who enjoy it and slowly, one by one, I lost my old friends in politics. Constructive criticism, at first welcome, soon grew sour compared with the sycophancy of those who had axes to grind and beds to feather. Power corrupts because it isolates and because in the modern world there is no room for the traditional fool of Shakespearian days.

So, as the years went by, I increasingly lost interest in politics and became more and more absorbed by the study of social change. India was an ideal subject for this study, especially since I could remember it way back to 1945, to the days of Punjabi villages without electricity, to the days of gorgeous maharajas, the days when Worli was a coconut grove and Indira Gandhi a very shy, much exploited and very lovable young woman.

The family life spent in India belongs to me; all I would like to add here is that had I lived those crucial years in any more developed country, it would not have been possible for me to become the sort of journalist I managed to be. I could go away as much as I did and to such remote places because I could count on the affectionate loyalty of wonderful servants; without their support in the home I would not have been able to gather the sort of material which gave me the knowledge to write the books I wrote once Maurice's career took me away from India.

Last but not least, indeed very far from least, India to me means the friends we made and their children. There is in India such a wealth of human warmth, such genuine concern for one's friends that one feels alone and cold almost everywhere else in the world, which is why, to me, India is my extended family.

~

TAYA ZINKIN was a prominent French-born journalist and author. She was married to the ICS officer and author Maurice Zinkin and was the India correspondent of the *Manchester Guardian, Le Monde* and the *Economist*. She wrote several books on India including *The Story of Gandhi*, and an autobiography, *French Memsahib*. She died in 2003.

VIII

My Indian Interlude

~

H.A.N. MEDD

BETWEEN ARCHITECTURAL WORK in New Delhi and expeditions into the interior, the spirit of the country—past and present —offered a rewarding experience.

Mine is not one of those British families which for generations had had one or more members serving in India. Thus, when, in 1945, after serving my articles, I joined the office of Sir Edwin Lutyens in London, it was because I was a great admirer of what I had seen of his work in England and not because he was in any way connected with India, which at that time meant nothing to me.

Both Sir Edwin Lutyens and Sir Herbert Baker had one or more resident representatives on the site in New Delhi ever since they had been engaged upon the new capital project; and when, purely by chance in the autumn of 1919, I happened to meet in the street one of Baker's men, who had recently returned from Delhi, and asked me if I would be interested in going out as Baker's assistant representative in Delhi, I jumped at it. Such was the fortuitous encounter which set me on the course I was to pursue for the best part of my working life.

Until then my experience of foreign countries had been confined to France and Italy. What could have been more exciting then, than to go and live in—not merely to visit— a country of whose culture, climate and people I knew practically nothing and to work on the greatest imperial project in history, swan-song of an empire, though, that it was destined to be?

In New Delhi

During the later years of the First World War, progress on the new capital had slowed down and the annual visits of Lutyens and Baker had been interrupted; it can therefore be imagined with what enthusiasm and anticipation they were resumed in 1919. The building of the Secretariat blocks, which were Baker's responsibility, had by then reached a little above the top of Raisina Hill, half the height of which had been blasted off to form the level platform of the government court. Though work on them was now accelerated throughout 1920, the chief concern of Baker and his staff was with the design of the Legislative Assembly Building with its three Chambers, the need for which had emerged from the Montague-Chelmsford Reforms. The circular design as eventually built was not the only solution tried and much work was done on another, though on the same site. The foundation stone with its trilingual inscription was laid by the Duke of Connaught in 1921.

It was found afterwards to have been set slightly in the wrong position and had to be lifted and relaid. I sometimes wonder whether the superstitious saw anything significant in the fact that other foundation stones besides this, including those of the new capital itself as laid by King George V near

the Durbar Amphitheatre and of the India Gate, had to be
taken up and reset after being ceremonially laid.

On Christmas Day 1919, it was urged upon me that I must
go and see Agra. 'By all means,' I said, 'but I just haven't got
the price.' Lutyens, always full of fun, said he would get an
advance from Malcolm Hailey, who was then the finance
member. The money was forthcoming, from whom I don't
remember, and on Boxing Day I set off by train. On the
journey I primed myself with the history of the Great Mughals
and though my first visit to the Taj Mahal was at the unromantic
hour of noon, I was never more impressed by the spirit of any
building than I was on stepping from the bright sunlight into
the semi-gloom of the cenotaph chamber. Purists may criticize
the design of the Taj in some respects and this was the view
of several eminent architects whom I took to see it in later
years; but for what it was intended to be—a monument to
a woman—it is supremely successful. On this occasion I also
visited Fatehpur Sikri, always a favourite of mine and it was
on that first excursion into India's past that was laid the
foundation of what has remained a life-long interest in Indian
history, archaeology and architecture, though I regret I have
left so much unseen.

HIMALAYAN INTERLUDE

I soon began to make Indian friends besides those connected
with my work. I well remember being taken to visit a
distinguished old gentleman, Nawab Younus Mirza, in his
fascinating house in the heart of Delhi city. In due course he
came to tea with me and when the time came for his evening
prayer, I was unable to produce a prayer-rug for him; however
a clean bath-towel met with approval. Another friend whom

I often used to visit and got to know very well was Rai Pandit Radha Krishna Bahadur, the curator of the Mathura Museum; together we visited many of the ancient sites in that historic area, some of which had not then been excavated.

It was in August 1920 that I had my first glimpse of the Himalayas. I arrived at dusk at Simla after an exciting motor-cycle ride from Delhi on which I encountered wolves near Panipat, was carried bodily across the Ghaggar river between Ambala and Kalka and just managed to accelerate away from the horns of an athletic hill cow, which took a dislike to me, on the hairpin bends near Kandaghat.

Architecturally there can be few places more appalling than Simla; the middle and late Victorian eras were a bad time in England itself for architectural quality and the great classical tradition, which had been invoked with considerable success a hundred years earlier in the plains, was hardly suitable for a hill climate, but it was not realized that there was an indigenous hill style using local materials, stone, base and overhanging upper storeys in timber, which could have been studied and adapted. With the exception of a few houses, the only decent building in Simla was Walter George's Council Chamber which in a later incarnation I was called upon to turn into offices—and spoiled.

We took every opportunity of studying Indian architecture, sometimes near at hand as when in 1923 we surveyed the tomb of Ghiasuddin at Tughlakabad, which owing to heavy monsoon rains was standing in a vast lake as it was originally intended to do.

Any architect travelling from Bombay to Delhi by the G.I.P. route has probably made a mental note of the fine old palace at Datia which beckons from its eminence not far from the railway track. In 1922, with Arthur Shoosmith, who was

Lutyens's representative on Government House, I determined to satisfy my curiosity and go and see it and was much impressed with its plan and three-dimensional idea.

It was there that I sampled a bed of nails and was somewhat disappointed; the nails were so close together and so blunt that it was really not uncomfortable.

Not far away, on the banks of the Betwa at Orchha, there is another palace by the builder of that at Datia. Bir Singh Deva Bundela, undoubted *badmash* though he was, certainly had the command of some excellent designers; his buildings, and there are said to be others, deserve to be the subject of a careful study.

Other expeditions included Sanchi, then recently very well restored, and to see the Besnagar column, near Bhilsa, that unique relic of an embassy from a Hellenistic kingdom in the Punjab in the second century BC, which entailed wading up to our middle across a river to get to it. Ajanta, where though the quality of the painting exceeded expectation, the quantity remaining was sadly reduced; Ellora, possibly the least expendable of India's sculptural heritage; Khajuraho, where the northern Indian type of temple, sometimes called Indo-Aryan, is seen at its best.

MEETING WITH JIM CORBETT

The object of these expeditions was not always architectural, since I began to develop other interests as well. The 'hills' had always been a magnet for me and not merely because they offered a respite from the heat of the plains. I used to think I would go and climb some worthwhile peak but the only time I got to the permanent snow at 13,000 feet on the Pindari glacier, I realized that an eighty-mile walk from

Almora was no substitute for proper acclimatization—for which I had no time.

Once, I got lost trying to make a short cut on the old Moradabad-Naini Tal Road, which had fallen into disuse and the bridges collapsed; however, I fetched up eventually at Kaladhungi and called on Jim Corbett. It was shortly after he had at last killed the Rudraprayag panther, the account of which is, I think, his best story. And what stories they are! Other writers have covered similar ground but with Corbett it is not the mere recital of hair-raising encounters but the emerging picture of the man himself with all his humanity and love of nature.

Another remarkable man whom I got to know well until his untimely death in 1940 was Raymond Grant-Govan, one of the most dynamic men I have ever met. His interests were not confined to his wide business activities; he did much to put Indian hockey and cricket on the map and civil aviation, especially the establishment of flying clubs, owed much to his energy and initiative. He had a house near the top of the Kulu valley, which it took him a day and half to reach from Delhi by road, and I well remember coming down with him from a Christmas party up there and stopping to inspect a strip of ground beside the Beas at Bajaura from which he thought, after the boulders had been removed, it might be possible for a D.H. Moth plane to land and take off—it proved to be so and Delhi to Kulu took two hours instead of days. I hope too that the Roshanara Club is still flourishing; it was his child.

ARCHITECTURE AND SHIKAR

My job in Delhi in those days was to receive, interpret and

if necessary, adapt the mass of drawings which were made in Sir Herbert Baker's office in London; there were very few features in the Secretariat and the Legislative buildings which I designed myself. However it was my good fortune to win the competitions for the designs of the Anglican Church of the Redemption and of the Roman Catholic Church in New Delhi, both of which are now cathedrals. With the arrival of Lord Irwin as Viceroy in 1926, the question of an Anglican church in New Delhi was reconsidered, a new and much better site was chosen and the foundation stone was laid the following year. Lord Irwin took a keen interest in the progress of the building and I found him very kindly to work with.

I had become a keen *shikari*; there were few better areas than the country eighty miles round Delhi for small game, which was what I was interested in. Many of my happiest memories of India are of those bright winter mornings on the jheels at Najafgarh, Nuh or Jhajjar. The Christmas holiday was a time for a camp or expedition, not always connected with shikar. I had a particularly good one in 1930–31 with Tim Blomfield, first by road to Jaipur where I was able to indulge another of my interests by browsing in the state library and examining, under guard, what is probably the finest Mughal manuscript book in existence, the Emperor Akbar's copy of the *Roznama*.

We then went on by Tonk, Bundi and Kotah and through the Mukandwara pass, where the British took such a pounding by Holkar in 1804, to the site near Mandasor of another battle nearly 1,300 years earlier which is marked by fine Gupta monuments. After another visit to Ellora and Ajanta, we had to return to Delhi by train after a motor smash due to a burst tyre.

The new capital as originally envisaged was now nearing completion and in April 1931 it was officially inaugurated; among those present was Lord Hardinge who had got special permission from the King to visit India again, which no ex-Viceroy was normally permitted to do; it was in his time twenty years previously that the project had been started. Lutyens and Baker and their staffs had done what they came to do and returned to England. I was sorry to leave the scene of so much interest and pleasure. However, for me personally the end was not yet, though I did not know it at the time. From 1931 to 1935, I was working in London largely on the drawings of the churches in Delhi, which were not finished when I left.

Rifle-shooting had always been one of my interests and during those years at home I pursued it regularly with the India Rifle Club at Bisley. In 1935 India won the Raja of Kolhapur's Imperial Challenge Cup with a record score, which has never since been bettered but only by one point in 1947, and that was only as the result of a challenge.

A shot had been signalled as an 'inner' but when examined through the powerful telescope was seen to be so close to the 'bull' line to be worth a challenge; this entailed the payment of a fine and the re-examination of the target, which resulted in it being declared a 'bull'. We had beaten Canada by one point!

Towards the end of 1935, the government of the Central Provinces decided to appoint an architect to design the High Court, which was to be built at Nagpur, largely on the initiative of Dr Raghavendra Rao. I applied for the post and was appointed and in November of that year I found myself back in the country which I thought I had left for good four years before.

I was in the CP only for four years, but in some respects they were the most interesting of all the time I had in India either before or later. The people were charming, the country interesting, so different from the northern plains, and the work was absorbing. But I was alone, isolated, there was not a soul with whom I could discuss a professional matter other than those of a structural nature which the PWD were able and willing to solve.

When in doubt on any architectural or aesthetic problem, I had to rely solely on my own resources. However, after a false start the site was finally settled and the foundation laid by Sir Hyde Gowan, the Governor at the time.

I have often wished that we could have used the Dholpur stone which we did at Delhi instead of the local stone from Saoner, which has gone black, but it would have been much more expensive. Besides the High Court there were a number of other jobs to be done; so I was kept pretty busy. I lived in a government bungalow called 'Land's End', and employed my spare time in making a garden there, which involved a good deal of excavation and levelling. Sir Gilbert Stone, the chief justice, was a keen gardener, but he lived on the floor of the valley with deep rich soil, whereas I was on a stony hill. He produced better flowers than I did but I used to say to him, 'Your garden will have returned to the jungle when mine still exists because it does not depend solely on surface treatment, but is in three dimensions with terraces, steps, etc.' I wonder what it is like now. Another keen gardener in Nagpur at that time was C.D. Deshmukh.

In the spring of 1939, R.T. Russell CIE, DSO, who had been Chief Architect to the Government of India almost from the commencement of New Delhi, decided to retire. It is not always realized what the new capital owed to him, for apart from the central buildings and a few houses, practically all the official buildings of the original city were designed by him and his staff. My work in Nagpur was nearing completion and I put in an application to succeed Russell, which was accepted. After a short leave in England I took up new duties in Delhi in September.

Second World War

The war had started but in India, as elsewhere, it got under way gradually and the enormous requirements in military and civil building which were subsequently found necessary could not be foreseen. The Army Headquarters had always occupied about a third of the south block of the Secretariat and when it did begin to expand it did so by extending itself at the expense of other departments. But the time came when additional space was needed and for reasons of easy communication this had to be nearby.

This process, with ever increasing momentum, went on till every open space, with the exception of Central Vista itself was built upon, no matter whether it was originally intended for building or as open space. Offices, barracks, hospitals, hostels and institutes of all sorts and of the shoddiest construction were rushed up at incredible speed. It was all supposed to be temporary and I was determined that not a single permanent tree, most of which were at least twenty-five years old, should be sacrificed to accommodate it. It was universally agreed that it should all come down after the emergency; some of it has, but more of it has been built since, sometimes in the wrong place, for example, the quarters for

MPs which I am told have been built under the trees of the avenue running north from Rashtrapati Bhavan, which should never have been considered as a building site. It was a sad time for me; I used to feel that though I had a good deal to do with the original New Delhi, I was now the principal instrument of spoiling it. Indulging in hindsight is unprofitable but if the coming of the Americans and SEAC could have been foreseen how much better it would have been to have built a war HQ designed as such, outside New Delhi.

There was a host of other problems to be dealt with, many not directly connected with the war effort, and the solution of them was often made difficult by the absence of any considered plan of how the city was to be expanded beyond the originally planned area, the limits of which had now been reached. After much delay a town-planner was recruited but, most unfortunately, he died before his master-plan was produced.

Of schemes elsewhere in India, the most important was the new Mint in Calcutta; the old Mint near the end of Howrah Bridge had done duty since 1826. A new site was found on Diamond Harbour Road and laid out, trees planted and some subsidiary buildings put up and much of the steel-work of the main building, which was to consist of a long, formal front concealing what was in effect a factory behind, was erected. Then came the threat of Japanese invasion and it was deemed advisable to transfer the whole project up country. There were not enough kilowatts available in Delhi so it was set down five miles east of Lahore where it could be powered from the Mandi hydro-electric grid. All the steel superstructure of the main building was dismantled and transported to Lahore, the intention being that after the war it should be taken back and work resumed in Calcutta. But things turned out differently, and after Partition the 'temporary' Mint found itself in Pakistan and is now the Pakistan Mint: luckily it was much better built than most so-called temporary buildings.

While in Lahore, in connection with the Mint, I became involved, much to my liking, in the repair and renovation of the great Badshahi Masjid. About this time too some anxiety arose regarding the stability of the Taj Mahal and a special committee, of which I was a member, was set up under Sardar Sir Teja Singh Malik who was then Chief Engineer, CPWD. The whole building was carefully surveyed and calculated by the mathematician, Khan Bahadur Muhammad Sulaiman. No serious failure was revealed, though there were many small cracks. The Taj Mahal is a brick building, of immense solidity and cased in white marble, much of which had been cramped together with iron, which had expanded and cracked the marble. During research into the history of the building an interesting document was unearthed in the Tonk state library; it was an eighteenth-century transcript of a seventeenth-century contemporary account of the actual building of the Taj and described its method of construction.

In 1945 it was realized that much additional permanent office building would be required in the centre of New Delhi and I was asked to make outline proposals for such development though much of the land was then occupied by temporary buildings. I then went home on leave and worked on my plan in the High Commissioner's office; when finished it was submitted to the Royal Fine Art Commission who, in their report to the Government of India, gave it general approval in principle.

During my leave I got married and returned to Delhi full of enthusiasm that now at last I would be able to do something worthwhile towards the permanent development of New Delhi, after all those years of having to clutter it up with shoddy buildings. In this I was destined to be disappointed; naturally enough things did not get going again very quickly after the war and before long, political turmoil and the shadow of Partition spread over the land. Work on the Mint in Calcutta was resumed eventually after I left, though the great front I had designed for Chunar stone was done in brick and plaster without reference to me—I have never seen it.

I retired in June 1947, but did not return to England till October as I thought it might be worthwhile to stay on and practise in India, but with the aftermath of Partition it became obvious that this would not be.

Though its termination coincided with the greatest upheaval in the country's history, viewed as a whole, my time in India was a most interesting and rewarding experience and one I shall never regret. To any young man going out to a foreign country, my advice is, 'Enter into the spirit of the country and do the things that it offers and don't sit down wishing you were at home.' This applies particularly to India which has more of interest to offer than most.

~

H.A.N. MEDD was an architect who entered the office of Sir Edwin Lutyens in 1915. He also worked closely with Sir Herbert Baker in New Delhi. He was Chief Architect to the Government of India from 1939 to 1947. He died in 1977.

IX

A Spell in Hindustan

~

PHILIP CROSLAND

CHINA WAS THE COUNTRY that really attracted me, but when I saw an advertisement in the *Times* for an editorial assistant for the *Statesman*, I applied for the job and got it. After all, I told myself, India was half-way to China, and since many of my forebears had served there, either in the army or as civilians, it was appropriate that I too should do a spell in Hindustan.

Arthur Moore, the editor, recruited me in October 1938 and, within a fortnight, I was on my way to Bombay on the *City of Canterbury*, a one-class boat, fare £40.

The passengers were a pleasant lot. There were several planters and their wives, a sprinkling of British and Indian businessmen, several young probationers for the Indian Police and a couple of subalterns of the Indian Army. In the close society of shipboard life, they all appeared to get along pretty well together and I could see no signs of those divisions, political and social, which were said to set Europeans apart from Indians, Europeans from other Europeans and Indians from Indians.

Fortunately these rather unpleasant attitudes did not apply in the *Statesman*, where colleagues in the newsroom and the reporters' room did their best to see that my education proceeded along more liberal lines. There were the retired academics like Wordsworth, the deputy editor, and B.B. Roy, a leader writer; the professionals whose lives had been spent in journalism like George Crawley, the news editor, Alec Reid, a dour, kind-hearted Scot who ran the newsroom, and A.D. Das Gupta, a quiet, gentle reporter; and those like Ian Stephens—who was to succeed Arthur Moore as editor when the latter was sacked early in the war—who had come to journalism from other trades.

A COSTLY CULT

B.B. Roy was always surrounded by a thick haze of cigar smoke. In a drawer of his desk he kept bundles of Burma cheroot tied in pink or yellow tape, which he was wont to press upon the newcomer with the remark that life only began after one had become familiar with 'the cult of the Burma cheroot.' I took his advice to heart and over the years it has cost me a great deal of money.

One of the most fascinating people I met at this time was the *Statesman*'s most famous outside contributor. This was Henry Newman, who under the pseudonym of Kim wrote a daily column of great popularity. Politics was barred in 'the Tent' where the action of 'Here and There', the title of Kim's column, took place, but every other topic under the Indian sun was discussed.

People wrote to Kim from all over the world—generals, policemen, tea-planters, engine-drivers, businessmen, clerks and shop assistants—and their letters provided most of the fabric for Kim's daily piece.

I was not happy in Calcutta and the fault was largely mine. I suspect that one reason was that the contrast between the England I had recently left and the City of Palaces was too great for me to reconcile easily. Another was that I was a little disappointed with India. I don't really know what I had expected, but it was something more 'romantic' than what Calcutta had to offer. Perhaps my notions of what India would be like had been shaped too strongly by *Kim*.

Another difficulty was my lack of understanding of the political complexities. I liked Indians. But I could not understand their preoccupation with politics. In a world where politics was meat and drink and indeed dominated life, it was my misfortune to be an apolitical animal.

TRANSFER TO DELHI

India was to give me another chance; after four months in Calcutta I was transferred to Delhi. Before I left the city I was to meet two famous Bengalis, Rabindranath Tagore and Subhas Chandra Bose.

I was presented to Tagore at a performance of one his plays in Calcutta. 'Presented' suggests a royal occasion, but it is the word which best describes our meeting. Tagore wore a black cloak and his silver hair was shoulder length. He was very regal in appearance and also very old and frail. Surrounding him were half a dozen beautiful young women students.

Subhas Chandra Bose I encountered at a house near Lansdowne Road at that most British of institutions, tea. He was one of several guests and the conversation across the tea cups was lively and spirited—and, of course, political.

I arrived in Delhi on a hot-weather morning with the Red Fort and Juma Masjid looming up out of the dust haze as the office car bore me along the road to New Delhi. In those days the Delhi office of the *Statesman* was regarded by those at the head office as an upcountry outpost, a sort of foreign legion fort to which were consigned those members of the staff redundant in Calcutta. One did not acquire *le cafard* at this outpost, one had it before one arrived; indeed, it was why one was sent there! Anyway, this was the popular theory.

But the Delhi office was a good place and every other member of the staff was a character. Dwarka Nath Kalhan, who later left the paper to join the *Hindustan Times*, was one of these. Tolerant and easy-going, he was one of the first friends I made in Delhi. Another was Kishen Pershad and his family, whose ancestors had been bankers to the Moghul court. At a time when old Delhi was old hat as an address and everyone was moving to the new city, the family clung to their fascinating old house in Chandni Chowk, where Kishen lives to this day.

I had not been long in Delhi before I discovered that I liked it very much. It conveyed such a tremendous sense of history. With its great monuments, Humayun's Tomb, the Purana Quila, the Lodhi tombs and the hundreds of ruins spread across the Delhi plain, it seemed to me to have been there for umpteen thousand years and conveyed the impression that it would still be there when everything else had perished.

A SENSE OF HISTORY

Pottering around Delhi's ruins was the nearest I ever came to 'culture activity'. There may have been a cultural life in the capital in the hot weather in those days, but if so it eluded me. After a few months, through my Indian friends, I even began to understand the political background better and to realize how these friends felt about swaraj.

A few years ago I remember reading a review in an Indian journal of a novel (by an Indian author who was also in the diplomatic service) in which the reviewer remarked that Mr X's heroes and heroines could not make up their minds whether they wanted swaraj or ballroom dancing. Whether true or not, I thought the comment very funny. However, my friends were in no such dilemma. They admired Britain and British institutions, they liked Britons as individuals, but all of them without exception looked forward to the day when India would be independent. I sympathized with this point of view and found it difficult to accept the view of the school of thought that said, 'Yes, of course India must be independent, but she is not ready for it yet.' Whenever I heard this dogma expounded I wondered whether we in Europe had ever been ready for our independence.

As if to underline this point we were suddenly at war in Europe and I joined the Indian Army. There was no talk of politics there, although the Blimps, beloved of Low and other cartoonists, were absent in the infantry regiment I joined.

Six years later, after an undistinguished military career that was compounded in almost equal proportions of hilarity and acute discomfort, I was back with the *Statesman* in a Calcutta preparing for Direct Action Day.

On that steamy August day in 1946, I watched the rioting from the roof of an officer's hotel.

Independence came the following year and I remember driving with a friend in an ancient motor car along the crowded roads.

India's freedom, I believe, benefited the British as much as it did Indians. It removed the last psychological impediment to uninhibited friendship between individuals of the two races and the Briton was enabled to relax and enjoy the country and the many good things it had to offer without the feeling that he was unwelcome. Overnight he ceased to be a ruler and became a friend.

The assassination of Mahatma Gandhi was another event which I remember vividly. The earliest report as they came over on the teleprinters said simply that an attempt had been made on his life. Later came the announcement with traumatic suddenness that he was dead. The night was one of the longest I have ever passed.

The Calcutta office was a purposeful place in those post-war days. The paper's reputation had been enhanced during the war years and particularly by its courageous reporting of the Bengal Famine. Ian Stephens, the editor, was an eccentric and complex personality who bicycled to the office in shorts and singlet and stood on his head for fun, combining his intellectualism with a strange admiration for fighter pilots, Pathans, Australians in the great outback, and other esoteric creatures.

Sudhindranath Dutta, the poet, was a member of the staff, and I do not believe I have ever met anyone with a greater sense of fun. His wife Bajeshwari shared this sense of humour. At their flat one met some of the most entertaining people in Calcutta—Victor Sasson and his brother Joe, Sunil Janah, Verrier Elwin, John Auden and his wife, the Emmersons and many others.

Verrier Elwin invariably travelled second class on the railways and affected the most unsahib-like attire. Arriving at

Sealdah station one morn, unshaven, cheroot in mouth, battered topee on his head, he was stopped by a Customs and Excise man who asked to inspect the contents of his suitcase. When he had finished, Verrier asked him why he had picked on him and was told, 'Sir, you are obviously not a first class European gentleman.'

COFFEE HOUSE

One of the great Calcutta institutions of that time was the Indian Coffee House in Chittaranjan Avenue, and since it was just across the road from the *Statesman* it was popular with members of the staff. It was divided into two sections, which were generally known as the House of Commons and the House of Lords.

In the Commons, your coffee was brought to you with the milk already in it; you merely added the sugar. In the Lords, milk, sugar and coffee were produced on a tray in their separate receptacles and the customer paid for this refinement.

In the Commons there was pandemonium. The Upper House was appropriately sedate. A table near the door was almost invariably occupied by the Chief Secretary to the West Bengal government, whose name I have forgotten, immersed in the *Statesman* crossword. In the centre of the room was a galaxy of talent from an advertising agency. One of their number would be Satyajit Ray, yet to find fame as a film-maker, but a quarter way through the making of *Pather Panchali*. Dilip Mukerjee and Chidananda Das Gupta would also be there. Another regular was a gentleman who bore an uncanny resemblance to the Russian dictator and was consequently known simply as 'Stalin'.

In the autumn of 1935 I was back in Delhi again, this time as news editor. It was like coming home. Post-war Calcutta was a vital and interesting place to be in, but I suffered from a sense of claustrophobia there. Delhi was the capital and with India's new-found independence was at one of the world's political crossroads.

It was a very different Delhi to the one I had known before the war. No one departed for Simla when the hot weather arrived. It was much less official. It was almost entirely Indian. There was a cultural life which had not existed before— mushairas, plays in English and Indian languages, art exhibitions and a new awareness of the country's arts and crafts.

In the hot weather, when polo, hunting and pig-sticking were temporarily in abeyance, the Army Equitation School held its Sunday morning rides in the countryside around Delhi, usually led by Colonel (now General) Sartaj Singh. My favourite ride was from the Palham Road to the tomb of Sultan Ghori, beyond the Kutb, where we usually had breakfast. Fishing was a gentler pastime, without the complication of a horse, which I also pursued.

In the north, every season has its own particular charm. The cold weather brings a profusion of flowers and the most wonderful climate in the world. The summer brings the pleasures of sleeping out and the sweetness of the kharbuza; the monsoon a profusion of mangoes. It is a cycle which never palls.

One phenomenon of the post-war Delhi scene which was with us irrespective of season was the diplomatic cocktail party. I do not suppose there has ever been a time when journalists have been so much sought after by the world of diplomacy. Indeed, it often seemed to me that diplomatic folk judged the success of their parties by the number of journalists who attended them!

This shows, I think, that the modern diplomat has also a public relations function to undertake. Not many years ago, in capitals throughout the world, the journalist could expect to get no further than beer with the butler in his pantry. A whisky and soda with the ambassador was beyond his place in the scheme of things.

I did not really appreciate the importance of the ambassadorial cocktail party circuit until one embassy cancelled its subscription to my paper (it bought six copies every day) because at one party it hosted no member of our staff turned up. It took us a month to jolly them out of the slough of depression and gloom into which they had apparently been plunged by our absence from their party!

When Evan Charlton became editor in Calcutta, I moved up to the resident editor's job in Delhi and after two years went down to Calcutta to do a short spell as Deputy Editor before becoming General Manager.

My time on the editorial side of the paper was as eventful as anything that has gone before. Of that period the memory which sticks most in my mind is of the preparations that had to be made in anticipation of possible air raids during the short war with Pakistan. Windows were blacked out, panes of glass were criss-crossed with brown paper to prevent broken glass flying about the place, blast walls were built, a wall of sandbags protected the main entrance to the office, and the staff were drilled in the business of taking cover in the event of air attack. The IAF station at Barrackpore saw action, but the measures we had taken in Calcutta were never put to the test.

My managerial job brought me into much closer contact with the men who were concerned with the nuts and bolts of the Indian newspaper industry. The experience was an enlightening one. Previously I had always been on the other side of the fence, and journalists, in India and elsewhere, tend to regard managerial members of the newspaper family with some misgiving. If journalists could run the newspapers, how quickly all problems would be solved!

In a world concerned with newsprint supplies, advertising rates and circulation figures, I made a number of good friends.

ON EXTENDED LEAVE

My time in India was cut short by devaluation, but my connection with the country and the many friends I made there has not ended. Scarcely a week goes by without a letter from India or a telephone call from someone passing through London from India. And despite the fact that my friends become more and more like Americans, with a devotion to a 'tight schedule' which is touching but un-Indian, some of them come to stay with me at my home in Portsmouth.

And like all Englishmen (and Scotsmen, Irishmen and Welshmen) who have lived in India and come to regard it with affection, I think of myself as temporarily absent, on extended leave, as it were, merely filling in time before that long return visit I have promised myself.

Political disagreements will, I have no doubt, sometimes disturb the relationship between India and Britain, but personal friendships are, I know, proof against such temporary inclemencies.

~

PHILIP CROSLAND started his journalistic career as an editorial assistant with *The Statesman* in 1938 in Calcutta. He was later transferred to Delhi. During the Second World War he joined the Indian Army. He resumed his career with *The Statesman,* becoming Resident Editor, then Deputy Editor and finally, General Manager.

X

The India I Love

~

J.A.K. MARTYN

I DO NOT THINK that I would ever have come to India if it had not been for that very remarkable German Jew, Kurt Hahn, who in 1936 founded a public school in the north of Scotland and later inspired the Outward Bound Schools. When I first knew him I was teaching history at Harrow and he was head of Salem, a school he had established on the shores of Lake Constance, based on the ideas of Plato and the principles of British public schools. After he had escaped from Nazi Germany, I drove him to Scotland on the journey that led to the founding of Gordonstoun. I longed to put his ideas into practice but at conservative Harrow I had no opportunity to do so. When I read in the *Times* that A.E. Foot of Eton had been appointed headmaster of a new public school to be opened for Indian boys at Dehra Dun, I offered to come with him and my offer was accepted. Foot had earlier been in touch with me about my experiences in taking a party of Harrow boys to help unemployed South Wales miners dig allotments. I had no previous interest in India; what interested me was the chance of starting a public school in a new environment.

While I was waiting for my passage to India I went around England, seeking advice. Lord Halifax (he was chairman of the committee that had selected Foot) said that the best way of getting support from Indians was to make them think that they had thought of your good ideas themselves. C.F. Andrews's contribution was not to keep people waiting on one's doorstep but to make oneself as accessible as possible; Edward Thomson (the novelist) warned me that my Indian pupils would lack the self-confidence of Harrow boys; perhaps they did at first but not for long.

A Wonderful Company

The *Mooltan* by which I travelled to India in February 1935, was full of returning ICS officers who were both encouraging and discouraging. They all agreed that India was a wonderful country, but many of them told me that Indians usually let one down. I presume they were thinking of those people (perhaps a little commoner in India than elsewhere), who being unable to say 'no', make promises that they cannot fulfil. Customs officers in Bombay were absolutely horrified to find from my passport that I had recently paid a visit to Russia. On 1 May, I had indeed stood in the Red Square and been quite carried away by the scenes of enthusiasm that accompanied the May Day Parade. The Customs officers wanted to open every one of my packing cases of books, but fortunately a friendly ICS officer persuaded them that it was not necessary.

In Bombay I learned that the opening of the school had been postponed from March till September, as the buildings were not ready. This gave me an opportunity to remedy to some extent my ignorance of India and in fact to fall under her mysterious spell.

I broke my journey north at Gwalior, to see the Scindia

School into which the Jagirdars' School had been converted a few years previously by F.G. Pearce. I was entranced by its romantic situation on the Fort and still remember a camp-fire against the backdrop of the ramparts and the sun setting across the distant plain. I was delighted when Pearce lent me Indian clothes, including a *safa*, to wear for dinner; but he confided to me that he found he got more respect if he stuck to Western dress.

AT SANTINIKETAN

Shortly afterwards I visited Santiniketan in his company, the visit coinciding with Spring Festival, when girls danced gracefully in a scented mango grove. The Poet told me that he had informed our founder that he did not approve of a school that would create an exclusive class. I on my part felt that the atmosphere of Santiniketan was, although very charming, rather precious and unpractical.

My tour continued to Benares, where I found the crowded ghats quite bewildering, but was impressed by the University and the Theosophical School. Thence to Allahabad, to call on Sem Higginbottom at the Agricultural Institute, before returning to Dehra Dun to spend a few weeks at the Language School in Landour trying to learn Urdu. I used to try to practise my little knowledge on social occasions but was never given a chance.

During my tour I had been very impressed by how welcome I was made to feel by all Indians I met, even very nationalistic Indians. In the summer I joined some friends for a trek in the Kagan and Kashmir. This was an enormous delight, and a Himalayan holiday became a regular feature of my life for many years to come. When limbs became stiffer, trout fishing took the place of mountaineering, but even then, in 1965 I reached the Base Camp on the Janoli Expedition, organized by the school.

The new school eventually opened on 10 September 1935, and came to be known as the Doon School. It was Arthur Foot who did the main planning, but luckily his ideas ran parallel to my own. I would not have been as bold as he was in trying to eliminate punishments, but we were equally keen on providing as wide a range as possible of activities that were creative and challenging.

The problem, as we saw it, was to create an atmosphere in which boys would learn the importance of truthfulness and public spirit at the same time as they acquired self-reliance and initiative. The school was far more ideally situated for expeditions than I had dared to hope, and before long many other masters keen on mountaineering had joined the school.

I have often been asked what was the difference between Indian boys and English boys and have always said that there was very little.

Life in the Doon School was absorbing and when the war came and some masters joined up, I then felt glad that I was not expected to go because I was so anxious to see that the school was established on the right lines. Sometimes I have regretted that I missed what would have been a broadening experience. The Doon School turned out to be almost all that I had hoped for and, although I had intended to stay for ten years, I stayed until it was time for me to retire. I cannot think of any other job that I would have been capable of doing which I should have preferred.

The Dehra Dun of 1935 seems incredibly remote today.

Quite a vivid example of this is perhaps that I bought a perfectly good Chevrolet for Rs 750. But, more importantly, all the officers at the IMA, where there were then about 250 cadets, were British (although Generals Shrinagesh and Som Dutt were to join shortly as Majors), and all the officers in the Gurkha Centres were also British and remained so until 1947; in fact they used to say that the Gurkhas would never serve under Indians, but I did not believe them.

OLDEST DAYS

Indians were not yet admitted to the Doon Club, and Foot, for that reason, did not join. He was married but I, as a bachelor, was not prepared to carry my disapproval of this exclusiveness so far. On Saturday nights we danced in tails and white ties, and when I went on leave in 1939 I had to buy a new tail-coat which I have never had a chance to wear.

There was in those days very little social contact between the British officers and the citizens of Dehra Dun, and this meant that the English masters at the Doon School found themselves living in two different social worlds. When Mrs Foot started wearing a sari for dinner in the privacy of her own home the news went round the horrified messes that she had 'gone native'. Foot used to insist on all masters wearing white suits with collars and ties, even in the hottest weather. Holdsworth was very anxious to discard his coat and tie. Eventually an Indian member of the staff got permission to come to school in Indian dress. Holdsworth, who had been in Peshawar, promptly started taking his classes disguised as a Pathan, complete with pugri but minus coat and tie. I began to wear a kurta and pyjamas in the evenings; I think that we may have felt that we were showing our sympathy with Indian aspirations. But I always had a vague feeling that if I travelled third class or dressed too disreputedly I would be letting the Empire down. 'Hippies' in those days could not have been imagined.

If the British officers of Dehra Dun looked somewhat sideways at the odd Englishmen in the Doon School, so too it seems did the benign government. When I wrote a letter to subscribe to the leftist Book Club, the police came round to search my bungalow while I was out riding and my letter never arrived. When the local officials read Foot's letters to his mother that a certain George was shortly to arrive, they decided that George must be a communist agent who must be intercepted. When they read that he had arrived escaping their notice, they were very surprised; but they need not have been, for he was the expected first-born.

Foot decided for family reasons that he would return to England in 1948 and I was asked to succeed him. When I was on leave in England, shortly before Independence, my friends mostly thought that I was making a mistake in staying on in India for they felt an Englishman's position would be rather uncomfortable. They could not have been more wrong.

AFTER INDEPENDENCE

I have found my life since 1947 much pleasanter than before. In the first place, although no one had previously ever done or said anything to make me feel at all unwelcome, from now on it was often made quite explicit that I was very welcome. Secondly, I was no longer living rather uncomfortably with my feet in two different social worlds. Overnight, the British officers disappeared and their places were taken by Indians who filled them with tremendous confidence and poise. Thirdly, almost overnight, a number of parents of boys in the school began to occupy positions of no little importance in the country. Guests at Founder's Days began to include Governors of states, Chiefs of Staff, Generals and Admirals, Secretaries to Government and Commissioners. Whether justifiably or not, this certainly created a feeling in us that the school was playing a more important part in the life of the country.

Visiting VIPs at this time would always assume that the school had become much more Indian since Independence, but actually it was not so. We had tried to make the school as Indian as we could from the beginning; before 1947 the boys wanted to give expression to their Indianness by wearing Indian clothes as often as possible and playing Indian music on their gramophones. After Independence this no longer seemed necessary and some boys even produced dinner jackets to wear on Saturday nights and Western pop became the rage.

Inevitably my closest contacts with Indians have been with the parents of boys in the school.

When I was a child my father was housemaster in one public school, and an uncle headmaster of another, and I remember 'parents' being spoken of with alarm and even horror. But I never felt like this at Doon School; after 1947 a number of parents took the initiative in getting on first name terms with me, a thing that I cannot imagine happening in the case of any of the headmasters that I studied or served under in England.

There are several reasons why I should have found the parents of our boys easy to get on with. Wasn't it Malcolm

Muggeridge who said that the only real Englishmen now left were to be found in Delhi? I think I know some of them.

Was the school as important an experiment as I used to like to think? I do not know. Tagore and many others had been opposed to it because it was inegalitarian; but in a country where equality would only be possible at a very low level of living, this criticism seems to me to lack substance. Assuming that it is beneficial to expose a growing boy at a formative time of his life to a wide variety of stimulating experiences, it is surely better that some should have this experience rather than none. Ideally they should be selected on merit but that would require heavy subsidies.

The Doon School boy has perhaps shown less public spirit than I had hoped, but I do not know that he is worse than young men from other backgrounds. It is easy to see why government service has become less attractive, not to mention politics, as a career. Good businessmen make their own contribution to the welfare of the country, and at a time when increased production is a vital necessity, this can be not unimportant. That there has been a great increase in the number of schools run on similar lines cannot be denied.

When I retired from the Doon School in 1966, I felt that as far as the school was concerned I should go elsewhere; but after thirty-five years I had grown roots and made many friends in Dehra Dun. Then there was the two Welham Schools, founded by Miss Oliphant who was matron in my house in the first term of the Doon School; there was the Cheshire Home with which I had been connected ever since Cheshire's first visit to Dehra Dun in 1956, and the Ryder Cheshire Home across the Rispana. As Managing Trustee of the Cheshire Home in India, I have had the interesting job of trying to maintain contact with all the fourteen Cheshire Homes in India.

The social problems of India are so enormous that it is easy for an individual to feel that there is nothing that he can do about them; but I have met very many people, who, under Cheshire's influence have discovered that it is very rewarding to do something even for a few people once one had learned to know them as individuals. And at Clement Town there is the Tibetan colony and a vocational training scheme in which I am involved. Even in retirement, life is full of several interests.

What does India mean to me? In the press recently, I have read statements by young visitors from the West that they have learned to admire Indian philosophy, religion and culture. If I am to be honest I must admit that my own love of India does less credit to me and to India. I cannot honestly say that I have made the necessary effort to make much progress in these respects, and that therefore my love of India is more because of what she is than what she has achieved.

Obviously, no one is expected to show his admiration for India by becoming a Hindu: the most that I should hope for is that my experiences have made me a better Christian.

COLOURFUL VARIETY

As I sit writing this in the gorgeous winter sunshine, that alone seems to be a sufficient reason to love India dearly, but of course there is much more to it than that, though it is not easy to say what. We all know that human life has been going on for thousands of years and in India one is always getting fascinating reminders of this. How wonderful is the great variety of human types; how liberating the sense of spaciousness in a country that stretches from the Himalayas to Kanya Kumari! Social life also is more spacious for me than in the West. This is partly because of the fabulous Indian spirit of hospitality and partly because the mechanics of entertaining are easier (more servants, etc.)

Not that there are no snags in Indian hospitality; some of it is aimed more at the honour acquired by the host than at the comfort of the guest; some of it is not without a background of favours hoped for: and I wish weddings were not so large and ostentatious. Another fly in the ointment that I cannot help mentioning is the uncooperative attitude normally to be found in petty officials. Why do individuals of a people normally so amiable and obliging become so unreasonable once they find themselves behind a desk? Is it that power goes to their heads, or does fear of making a wrong decision paralyse their faculties; or is it just malnutrition? These are, however, no more than minor annoyances in a background to living that has a rich fascination which I have never been able fully to explain.

～

J.A.K. Martyn was the first Deputy Headmaster and the second Headmaster of the Doon School. He came to India in 1935 and visited Santiniketan and the Agricultural Institute at Allahabad before taking up his post at the Doon School. After India's independence he stayed on as Headmaster of the school.

XI

India Calling

~

LEONARD MARSLAND GANDER

INDIA CHANGED THE WHOLE course of my life, my habits and my hopes. She educated me and nearly killed me, alternately frustrated and profoundly depressed me, then inspired me to fresh ambitions and infused me with new ideas.

I grope for the apt word to describe the radical upset of my English way of life caused when I was astonishingly and unexpectedly appointed by the late Sir Stanley Reed, one time Editor of the *Times of India*, to the post of Chief Reporter early in 1924. Dramatic, exciting, traumatic. They are all too hackneyed, too inadequate.

At the time I had completed a four-year apprenticeship on an East London bi-weekly called the *Stratford Express* and was earning £4. 5s a week. I was desperate for a change, almost suicidally so. After six years, somehow I had to break away from the limited orbit of suburban affairs, inquests, local concerts, police courts, petty fires, council meetings. But I had no desire whatever to go to India. I had heard of that vast remote country, part of the Empire on which the sun never set and I thought how lucky the Indians were to be ruled by a race so indulgent and so gifted as the British. Forgive me; I have to tell the truth.

First Obsession

The fact is that my education by English standards had been somewhat sketchy and mostly free. I did not go to a public school or a university. I went to East End elementary schools; then won a small scholarship by the skin of my teeth to a much better school and took home the £10 bursary in triumph to my adoring mother. Then an elder brother paid for me to go to the City of London College, a specialized college mainly concerned with equipping boys and girls for office work.

Father had died. There was nobody to stop me. So at sixteen, for some extraordinary reason, I announced to an astonished but totally indifferent world that I was fed up with school examinations—did not want 'failed BA' after my name or any other initials, except perhaps the VC. I was going to be a journalist. No one in the family had ever been connected with newspapers and it is extremely difficult to explain my obsession.

But it was so difficult to get a newspaper job. I must have written to every paper in the United Kingdom. Those that took the trouble to reply gave me a polite brush off. But I was helped by one thing. It was August 1918, towards the end of the First World War, and man-power was running low. So eventually I got started on the *Stratford Express*.

Though on the doorstep of Central London, so to speak, to get a job in a London paper without proper provincial experience seemed impossible. I had refusal after refusal, rebuff after rebuff. Once I wrote to my hero Bernard Shaw to ask his advice. Shaw answered everything; his correspondence was prodigious and his postcards with the magic initials 'G.B.S.' were famous. Incidentally, I have what I believe to be the last one he wrote at ninety-four in 1950 but that is another story, as Kipling said.

Anyway, Shaw said: 'Stick to your local paper until you can obtain a footing in Fleet Street through friends or acquaintances.' This didn't satisfy me at all. One day I saw a small advertisement in the *Daily News* for a reporter on an Indian newspaper. It didn't say what paper or where. India? I had heard about the Mutiny and the Black Hole of Calcutta: about John Company and how Clive with small forces was alleged to have routed huge armies; about maharajas and fakirs; Kipling, cobras, snake-charmers and elephants with fantastic memories, weird creatures which I had also seen at the zoo.

BORI BUNDER CALLING

Above all, I had heard about the terrific heat. It didn't attract me at all. But the advertisement fascinated me and I wondered whether I would have the courage to accept this job, never dreaming that, having made the supreme sacrifice of applying, I might not get it. So with nervous reluctant fingers I wrote out my application. It was a staggering shock to my ego when I received no reply. Not a sausage. Not even a bare acknowledgment.

Then I made one of my periodical sorties into Fleet Street to receive the usual brush off from the *Times*, the *Telegraph*, the *Daily Mail*, the *Daily Express* and the *Daily News*. How the hell did anybody get started, I wondered? I was wandering disconsolately down the street when I noticed on an upper office window the words '*Times of India*, Bombay'. Well, better than the Black Hole of Calcutta, perhaps. Maybe it was the paper that didn't answer my letter, I thought.

So I raced up a narrow dingy staircase, burst breathless into an outer office and demanded to see the manager. Strange to say I succeeded, but then the manager was an unusual person—W.T. (Skipper) Coulton. 'Do you know anything about India?' 'No, sir.' 'What is your experience?' I told him. Well, to cut it short he referred me to Sir Stanley Reed whose idea was to find a young man (I was twenty-one) who would make India his life work.

So I got the job on a fabulous salary of Rs 500 a month, then the equivalent of £37 10s, more than twice what I was paid by the *Stratford Express* with the promise of the added privilege—a doubtful one I found—of living rent-free over the office at Bori Bunder.

I am conceited enough to believe that Sir Stanley Reed did not make a mistake about character or ability, but I think he was mistaken about my qualifications. I believe that he thought I lived and worked in Stratford-upon-Avon and was therefore in some rather obscure way connected with the Bard of Avon, William Shakespeare; he also thought that the City of London College was a pucca public school, confusing it with the City of London School.

So in March 1924, after a glorious and hilarious voyage, first-class, in the British India ship *S.S. Manela*, with Sandhurst boys freshly commissioned to the Indian Army as high-spirited boon companions, I arrived in Bombay. It was a shock, a grievous shock.

All night the *Manela* lay off the seething city with its phosphorescent glow and foetid air. I lay tossing sleepless in my bunk, sweating profusely and beginning to wonder whether I had not made a terrible mistake. The rise in temperature was from 40 Fahrenheit at Tilbury to 90; there was a peculiar smell of staleness everywhere, of ordure and of humanity in the mass, of burning and of incense—or so it seemed to me.

In the morning, when we docked, things were worse. All my pleasant companions of the voyage hurriedly disappeared. Peacock, the sub-editor who was supposed to meet me, hadn't turned up. Perhaps this was just as well. James Peacock, as I discovered later, was a debauched Scot from the *Glasgow Herald*, a man with thick pebble glasses, lank black hair, a bulging forehead, ill-fitting false teeth, and an unhealthy freckled complexion. He was also, I must hasten to add, a man of an exceptionally generous disposition, a clever journalist, and one who could write blank verse with Bardic facility. Anyway, he had had one of his habitual nights 'down the road' (which meant Grant Road, the brothel quarter) and he was *nai hai*. Nursing his hangover he turned up too late. I found my own way, a deeply worried youth, to the *Times of India* at Bori Bunder, in a gharry, a carriage drawn by a half-starved horse.

The East End of London from where I had come was no paradise, but the poverty, disease and despair were hidden behind the brick walls. First glimpses of Bombay appalled me and I suffered from disastrous home-sickness. But when I first met my Indian reporters my heart lightened; I felt a warming glow of surprise and admiration. I didn't speak one word of their languages; they all spoke and wrote English. It is true that I spoke and wrote in better English than they did, but then it was my native tongue.

I wondered how on earth did I come to be put in charge of this eminently civilized, well-educated, polite and amenable body of men? They were well-trained in reporting, too.

I marvelled at the accident of birth and the freak of history which had put me in charge. But above all I wondered how it was that this artistic, imaginative race could not organize

itself a bit better to abolish the poverty, the sickness and the
mass misery. Why was there so much illiteracy, such grinding
poverty?

After the lapse of forty-six years, I still have no ready
answer. Caste system? The British had a caste system all their
own. I could join the Gymkhana Club because I was on the
editorial staff of the *Times* but our printers had to be content
with the inferior Commercial Gymkhana. Incidentally in
England I hadn't belonged to any club and was certainly not
qualified for the Atheneum. By the way, Indians couldn't join
the Gymkhana or the Commercial version of it either.

Superstition? Well, my amiable senior reporter, Framroze,
dabbled in astrology, so I asked him to prepare my horoscope.
I have it still and I don't believe a word of it. But he predicted
my death in an accident in 1971, so will the editor of *Illustrated
Weekly* please pay me quickly for this, just in case?

Mix up of races? What race could be more mixed than the
British? Religion? We've had our quarrels but most people
now don't have one. It must be the climate.

Of Things Past

I learnt to drink and that cheered me up considerably. I still
think pleasurably of those genial circles around tables on the
Gymkhana lawn with a moon sailing across a black velvet sky.
It was the form to ask for specific brands of whisky and I
picked on Cockburn Campbell. Not that I could distinguish an
anna's worth of difference between them all but the name
sounded good. I joined the Bombay Light Horse and hunted
jackals with them—a sport in the fox-hunting variation that
in England would have been far beyond my means.

But I did, by Fleet Street standards, a colossal amount of work, especially when left in charge of the *Illustrated Weekly*, in those days almost a one-man band.

I reported Gandhi's speeches, particularly admiring his smiling aplomb and the convenient fact that he usually presented me with a typewritten copy of his utterances. But I thought of him as a subversive influence and a rebel. Years later, during the war, I had fixed up an interview with him but arrived at his Malabar Hill residence only to find that he had just been arrested and I, wearing the hated British uniform, was in the middle of a hostile crowd.

But I have always found that the text my mother put up on the wall is a magic formula. 'A soft answer turneth away wrath but grievous words stir up anger.' I harangued the crowd—those that spoke English—and they let me go to tell the world about the arrest. A wise decision.

Work and that bloody climate eventually brought me down because, as I discovered on my second visit, I hadn't drunk enough whisky. In the war years, thanks to whisky, I had no illness worth mentioning.

So, in the 1920s, after various recurring illnesses—malaria, dysentery, the lot—caused by idiotic overwork, the drastic change of diet and the heat, I eventually found myself in St. George's Hospital with a liver abscess. At last, a chastened bag of bones, I was packed off back to England, only to find when I arrived that I didn't like it any more. I longed for the warmth, for the strange 'kuch perwanai' nonchalance and unjustified gaiety of India and above all, I ruminated regretfully over those delectable Anglo-Indian girls.

My first two years made impressions so deep and lasting that I find it impossible to express them in words. While most of my colleagues and companions were content to eat, drink and indulge in any kind of sport, outdoor or indoor, that was available, I was determined to explore the architectural splendours, to see the Taj, the noble Moghul buildings, to visit the Simla of Kipling, to learn the language, to understand Hinduism and the Muslim teachings. Naturally I failed in all this. My Hindustani is a joke. But I believe that my written guides to the Taj Mahal and to Fatehpur Sikri are still in circulation——they ought to be.

I wish I could make coherent and constructive comments on the mysticism, the politics, the religions, the wild outbursts of emotionalism that made up and still make up part of the complex mosaic of Indian life. I cannot. It is too confusing, too sprawling. On my first stay I was preoccupied with the demands of daily journalism. During the war when, as a war correspondent, I had more time, more money, I was still intent on the targets of news stories. Journalism and study do not mix.

What does India mean to me now? First, it means a huge variegated subcontinent of infinite possibilities, with natural resources that still remain to be exploited effectively for the benefit of the majority; a country that ought to be a happy homogenous whole, ruthlessly divided into two countries by the ambitions of rival politicians; a country that has bred some of the finest architects and the most brilliant artists and thinkers that the world has ever known; a country on which the indulgent British made some impression while failing utterly to solve its problems of over-population, hunger and disease, a country where, despite the enlightened teachings of Gandhi and many others, religious bigotry and misguided, narrow patriotism still persist.

But it is a glimpse of the obvious that the British first went to India to exploit it commercially. The nabobs, rich and liverish, duly retired to Cheltenham and elsewhere with their fortunes to be puppets in Vanity Fair. Few ever thought of making India their home. Certainly I didn't, for chronic home-sickness was my constant ailment. But I didn't return with a fortune: with £300 to be precise and it is worth mentioning the remarkable fact that in 1926 I was offered this sum—my meagre savings—in gold sovereigns. It was cheaper to take the gold than pay the bank charges.

VENGEANCE OF TIME

Now the vengeance of time has turned the tables. It is the Indians and Pakistanis who are flocking to England to benefit from our higher standards of living, fuller employment and the many benefits of our superior social organization. The exploiters, in a way, are now the exploited. And it is fair enough, except that this is a small country by comparison with the great subcontinent and we too have our problems of ignorant race prejudice, housing shortages, inflation, political conflict. But who would man our hospitals and our transport system and perform many of the lower paid jobs in industry if we had no immigrants?

The editor of the *Weekly* asks me about my Indian friends. I shall still count him as one if he uses this article unchanged. I like to think that everybody I met were my friends—my bearers, the coolies, above all the reporters of the *Times*. I think still with immense sorrow and regret of my first bearer, an old man past the job really, who warned me repeatedly about the evils of drink and who went back to his village to die. I think of Mahomed, one of his successors, who stood in tears by the lake at Gwalior when his sahib went off never to return. Never? Well, Mahomed went back to Maiden's at Delhi, got out his praying mat and sure enough I turned up again. Allah be praised.

I think of the numerous people I met at the High Commission in London—moody, awkward, outspoken and brilliantly versatile Krishna Menon, and Gandhi, Nehru, Mrs Naidu.... Well, really only acquaintances.

The Maharaja of Baroda sends me a Christmas card every year. Jamal Kidwai and his charming delicate wife I haven't heard of for years. Well, bless them all.

When I went to India I moved from a pond to an ocean; from a lower middle class suburbia to a world of administrators, soldiers, statesmen, first-class journalists, dreamers, philosophers and artists—professionally I owe India an immense debt. I could have done without the liver abscess, but after all I haven't had a day's illness worth mentioning since and when I went to a Bombay dinner a few years ago, there were five old 'koi hais' at the top table, all in their mid-nineties.

~

LEONARD MARSLAND GANDER was a well-known journalist and wartime correspondent for *The Daily Telegraph*. He came to India in 1924 to join the *Times of India* and also did a stint in the *Illustrated Weekly*. He is the author of several books namely *Long Road to Leros*, *After These Many Quests: Autobiographical Reminisences* and *Television for All*. He died in 1986.

XII

A Long Love Affair

~

PEGGY HOLROYDE

BEYOND THE IMMEDIATE convulsive impact of poverty, the eternal appeal of India, lies in her rich heritage of culture. A country of such creative genius is destined to survive for all time.

Looking back, a generation wiser, it all appears as though it was meant to be. Indians, of course, would say it was in my karma. Harindranath Chattopadhya once cornered me with his flamboyant poetic manner and asserted that I had been born in India before—but how was I ever to have envisaged that in 1942 at the impressionable age of eighteen.

I was in America at the time, a student at the American Cambridge—Radcliffe College—by dint of my father having been sent on a wartime Admiralty delegation to New York. Soon after my arrival I was feeling homesick in an American coffee house just off Harvard Square when I heard an English voice amid the welter of fast-firing American accents. Although being in total rebellion against the Englishness of myself even then, I leant across the table towards the tall, lean man and the plump little woman. It turned out to be H.N. Spalding and his wife, Nellie. From that moment, unbeknown to me, the foundations were being laid for a pathway that has stretched with astonishing directness through my life into India and out again—and now, with yet another characteristic Indian turn of the cycle because of my commitment to race relations in the north of England and the work which so involves me with Asians in our midst, promises to return me to Indian soil (God willing) this autumn.

THE THEOSOPHICAL CULT

In my generation, the cult with American students was not pot, Zen Buddhism and Maharishis, but Theosophy and Annie Besant.

H.N., as Spalding was called, was blunt and acute. 'Throw her out of the window,' he asserted. 'Go to the sources. Read the Upanishads.'

He gave me a translation from one of his own books on Eastern religions and I began wrestling with thoughts I had never conceived could exist. And then he put a copy in my hands of Dr Radhakrishnan's The Hindu View of Life.

H.N. was stranded at Harvard during the war but the pattern he laid on my life was irrevocable. No sooner had I got my degree than I found myself back home and married. By 1946 Derek, my husband, was at Oxford himself, at Brasenose, H.N.'s old college, and H.N. was there with his philosopher brother K.J. Spalding. He was busily occupied with the setting up of the Spalding Trust and the Chair of Eastern Religions. The first incumbent of this chair was Dr Sarvapalli Radhakrishnan. Without even a conscious thought that I would, or could, ever go to India, I studied under him, and to my constant astonishment I managed somehow in my crass youthful aplomb to write a paper on 'Action and

Contemplation'. How I could have known anything of contemplation I do not know, considering I had by then a very lively eighteen-month-old baby, a husband and a huge university home to look after. Perhaps it was my longing for that joyous state of being that made me write with such conviction on the subject. There is nothing like the hard dogmatism of domestics to hone the mind to a proper intellectual appreciation of a subject.

Derek went into the Overseas Services of the BBC—and then it was 1953 and there lay before him the chance to go as Representative to the USA or to India. We chose India.

That can be said to be the only conscious decision, an act of irrational choice, in the whole unfolding of these stepping stones to the point where now in my constant lecturing and writing in England about India, her culture, religions and background, I am increasingly being asked if I am Hindu.

REALITY AND TRUTH

Westerners have asked me times without count why it is that I do not get disillusioned in my long love affair with India. I laugh and shrug my shoulders. Is it necessary to get disillusioned with the truth?

I have seen and known the worst about India—the suppurating lepers and beggars laid out like cadavers at the great Kumbh Mela when I saw 400 people trampled to death at the Sangam area in the 1950s; and the sadhus leering at me at the Kurukshetra moon-eclipse festival with lemons hooked into their skin, or iron bars stuck through their cheeks to silence them; I have been thrust out of temples rudely by fat pandits at Srirangam in Tamil Nadu (a salutary piece of poetic justice because only then did I feel the emotional identification with Indians who had in like manner been excluded from the English Club); and I have known the burning exasperation to the point of wishful skull-bashing when I have come up against the impregnable wall of Indian bureaucracy. (I once had to retrieve an unaccompanied suitcase from the customs office in Delhi, a three-day process, which literally reduced me to a gibbering state of tears and malevolence.)

I have seen stupidities, been badgered with opportunist requests, had my privacy invaded perpetually until I longed to curl up into a yogic trance, conveniently opting out—and longed for the mirage of an English spring day and the smell of damp primroses when that pewter sun in a leaden sky has throbbed to the very core of me while stranded at the bridge of boats at Gurmukteshwara. And I have watched our car slowly sink in a river while a Hindu priest stood under his immense umbrella, not lifting a hand to help in our struggle.

But India, that entity that goes beyond even its inhabitants, is more than its immediate convulsive impact. And I am grateful that circumstance has given me that breathing space to digest India with a lifetime's engagement, both in India and here in Britain. And ever since that moment in Kasauli when looking down on the plains to Chandigarh, leaning against a rock in the burning sun, I had a flashing sense of merging with all that surrounded me—the shepherd boy and his flute as he wandered after his goats, the splash of red minivets, and the swish of the deodar branches—I have really known what true yoga must attain, that total sense of vibrant oneness that now is sought so superficially through hallucinatory drugs.

A NEW BIRTH

India has always given me this acute sense of awareness, as though breathed in with the very atmosphere. I landed in Bombay in 1953. As the liner swayed at anchor offshore the waft of spices and dust, jasmine and drains, humidity and lingering malodours assailed me with that intangible sense of expectancy that ran through my body like an electric current. And this was to bring me new birth. Meteors streaked across the stardust, a late moon slipped over onto its fattened side and my universe expanded dramatically into another dimension. India had taken over, and somewhere in the deep recesses of my interior self I came 'home'.

If I say that it was a spiritual experience, I am only too aware within my own Anglo-Saxon ancestry of the signals that this word sends out.

But first I have to say one thing: within thirty-six hours of reaching our home in New Delhi, the night before Divali, I had been transported into the glittering world of Rashtrapati Bhavan amid the sparkling brocades, the vibrant reds and scarlets and golds of the Bodyguard Cavalry, and the austere white of Gandhian khadi to hear a grand sammelan of music. Dr Narayana Menon had made a truly imaginative gesture for both my husband and myself—he had opened the door (again symbolic) into the shimmering expanse of ragas and raginis with Bismillah Khan wringing a yearning pathos out of his shehnai and the late B.V. Paluskar with his sensuous voice tearing down the shreds of that last superimposed English inhibition that was not really part of our national nature until recent times. We did not breed Shakespeare for nothing, nor

John Donne, Thomas Traherne and all the Romantic poets
(which to my chagrin as an Eng. Lit. graduate, my Indian
friends can quote more word perfect than myself).

America, thank goodness, had undone much of my own
respectable and stern upbringing in that archetypal school,
Roedean, but the evocative pull and twist on my heart strings
that night, and the sense of liberation that mingled with this,
as I listened to those melodic intricacies, united the final cords
as the showers of *swara* and *shruti* worked their magic. Kipling,
reintroduced to me piquantly enough in Simla by Chalapathi
Rau, when the Press Commission was sitting in 1954, came
into new focus as one of the more sensitive writers of the
Indian scene when all the jingoistic poems are brushed aside,
for he once wrote as though melting at the edges in the Indian
climate: 'My English years fell away, nor ever, I think, came
back in full strength.'

Because of this characteristic quality of warm sentiment,
the overwhelming tactile sensuousness of India, and the
exhilaration of Indian friendship (remarked upon by all
nationalities), many a European takes the false notion that
India is all emotion without firmness of purpose, as though
the character had a soft aspect thereby. I was to find that
night a key to the India I came to love, first by instinct as a
woman does, to know later by intellect, and so finally to
respect with a force that nothing can ever shift, even should
the elements of extreme obscurantism and backward-looking
Hinduism that begin to thrust out their tentacles into the
body politic again, ever take over—and God forbid that this
should ever be. Indians are not by nature bigots, and the very
central core of their whole way of life, the Gita, explicitly

demands self-discipline of a high order.

In the music, and later the dance, and then in all the aspects of artistic expression of the Indian spirit, I found what I had encountered with the full impact of that magnetic first time, the disciplined sensuousness, emotion that was shaped and carved by astonishing intellectual calibre, the rugged training that even our own character-building theoreticians would doff a cap to.

CREATIVE VITALITY

No nation is finished that can produce people of such creative vitality as the multitude of Indian musicians whom we came to know as such warm and responsive friends.

Through the music I began to see come alive what I had only dealt with in mental terms when I had read those original Hindu books and had studied the *Bhagvad Gita* in an academic way. And this brings me back to the spiritual. Despite all that Mr Nirad Chaudhuri has ever said about the Hindu mind and the failure of the British ever to understand it, I count myself fortunate that I am a woman—and can therefore disagree with him, because the very feminine part of my being found a liberation within Hindu thought that I had not found in my own Christian upbringing, albeit this had been conventional and institutional.

And I must make my quite valid declaration as a woman as to why the Hindu mind is not totally inaccessible to a Westerner. For one thing it taught me to accept my feminine nature—and this was not always so. My American education had stirred that militant feminism which was in my temperament, and I was a muted woman liberationist before time. Consequently, I have for all these years of growth been ill at ease with myself, a woman longing to be a man. It was one of my Indian friends who once put me on the spot by saying quite casually that I had a man's mind in a woman's body. But India in a strangely oblique way has made me whole.

Despite the deadwood of at least forty centuries of man-made development, and despite the lazy thinking of Westerners when they embrace Indian mysticism and turn it into an esoteric cult, I find there are basic assumptions in the abstract metaphysics of Hinduism that are so fundamentally scientific in conception that they retain this astonishing capacity of appeal in all ages, no matter how modern. One of these logical and coherent views of creation (biologically correct, into the bargain) which spills over the boundaries of Hinduism into the syncretic and comprehensive attitudes of Indian culture is the concept of the creative Brahman as male/female energy —the Siva-Sakti balance in all creative matter which has led automatically also into secular life to a comprehensiveness of attitude to the male/female roles in the socio-political areas of life. This came to mind only recently when I was reading one of the more aggressive and, therefore, exaggerated books by a leader of the American woman's lib movement.

'God is Male,' she declares. 'We cannot therefore accept God.' This forces me to chuckle when I think of the Indian view of life and the imagery that has kept it evergreen in the Indian consciousness—the essential equality of creative energy, in fine equipoise between each male Deva and each female Devi. Each Radha, Parvati, Uma, Lakshmi, Durga, Kali and Saraswati complementing in her own symbolic aspect that of God, by whichever name He is worshipped.

How can one ever spell out truly the innermost impulses that bind one's being so that when an Indian crosses my path that quivering sense of identity is stirred again ... and again ... and again? India is all things—paradoxical until most Europeans give up the attempt to understand in the mind and forget to use the heart, chameleon-quick in changing just at the point when one thought one had grasped tangible feet.

She is princely rich and peasant poor, warm of heart yet inexplicably cruel, painfully beautiful and harsh, puzzling to the Greek logic of mind yet clear in immediate flashes as the frosted ice on the far reaches of the Himalayas. She is funny with ridiculous solemnity, demanding of patience, bound by an exasperating rigidity of ritual which created the ancient *shastras* yet flexible at the final point of despair, and tolerant in a unique way of all beliefs. She sprawls like formless chaos and her people seem to be in a constant state of flux, coming and going in torrential flood and reforming again, reviving after each gigantic cultural invasion.

India is as touchingly and maddeningly sensitive as an adolescent coming young and fresh into a technological century, and yet we begin to look again to her old, old wisdom, old as her mountain ridges buckling into the earth like pre-historic brontosaurean monsters.

THE NEED FOR SENTIMENT

I can be accused of waxing lyrical. Once I might have minded. Now I don't care. I have lived through an era and so have my children, where everything had to speak the language of realpolitik, where literature has been couched in terms of the brutal, the ugly, the solitary human condition of alienation not only from fellow men but the universe also, and where words also have been pruned back to the brevity of Beckett. We have been afraid of sentiment, and we have been suspicious of myth, and we have been alienated from the poetic.

Increasingly, there are signs of sheer tiredness and irritation at the sterility of all this negation. The young are reading Tolkein's *The Lord of the Rings* to such an extent that it is a modern classic ahead of its time (with nearly a thousand pages, interspersed with lengthy descriptive passages and heavy with imagery). Poetry is returning to university campuses, and religion is delicately treading into the pop-song world. George Harrison's 'My Sweet Lord' still remains the number-one record with its Alleluia chorus and Hare Krishna, Guru Brahm, Guru Vishnu chanting. 'Quintessence', another leading intellectual group, have only just brought out an LP called 'Dive Deep', based entirely on the chant 'Jai Ram'.

One begins to sense that people are sick of the easy commercial message, scientific arrogance, the superficiality of politics as we know them at the moment. Life is too intricate. The world of the tangible can give few solutions to the very real mess in which we all find ourselves. Ivan Illich, said to be one of the great Catholic thinkers of our time, has said: 'I am for those who want to deepen life rather than lengthen it.'

This is the way India's traditional thinking has always wisely led. This is the way the stepping stones of my own life have directed me into the unknown—into India where, to paraphrase Tagore's most beautiful poem, messengers greet me with tidings from unknown skies: and I know that, of a sudden, the happy moment will arise when I shall see.

~

PEGGY HOLROYDE was married to Derek Holroyde of the BBC who was posted in Delhi. Her great passion was classical Indian music and she wrote an acclaimed book on the subject, *Indian Music (1972)*. She has also written *An ABC of Indian Culture: A Personal Padayatra of Half a Century Into India* (2007).

XIII

From British Raj to Stri-Rajya

~

ARTHUR HUGHES

MY FIRST REACTION when I am asked why I have stayed in India
for the last forty-three years is to retort: 'Ask those who
have been here longer.' Why not approach Edmund Gibson in
Ramgarh, or Bill Williams in Roorkee? These two and the late
Norah Richards in Kangra (who died early this year) were
born in the nineteenth century and resident here since they
were young. In comparison with them I am almost a
newcomer. Each of them, too, has a concrete interest in life
and work in India: Norah Richards was involved with drama;
'Burra' Gibson in his farm; and Bill Williams had a very
concrete interest in roads and buildings. I have no such enduring
interest, since I have become a teacher of the young only in
later years, after spending half my Indian life as a government
servant. A near half-century of experience—learning, loving
and teaching ... and a yearning, by the waters of the Ganga,
to be born in India—if there is rebirth.

During that half of my life, it is true, I saw a lot of unruly
youngsters (nowadays they call them Naxalites) and exigent
trade-unionists, in and around Calcutta. Even in those days,

Calcutta was very seldom quiet, at least in the areas I knew best, Dum Dum and Howrah, Budge Budge and Barrackpore, Naihati and Chinsura. I have lived or stayed in them all, and can still, I hope, find old acquaintances if I venture into the by-lanes, away from the clashing crowds and the roar of the traffic on the main roads.

That part of my life made a suitable prelude to the job of a schoolmaster. I now enjoy the crescendo of noise made by five hundred boys just let out of school, the cheerful buzz of conversation in the common dining hall, and even the massed roar of the rival crowds at an inter-house football match. In fact I find it all rather tranquilizing, and suggest my way of life as a detensifier to the harried executives of Bom-Cal-Del.

A LOVE AFFAIR

Anyway, let me try and answer the question of what India means to me. I suppose that the shortest—and therefore the simplest—answer I can give is to call it a love affair, which began on the eleventh day of December, 1927, the day I set foot in India, and has continued ever since. Like most love affairs, it began slowly, with some doubts, then worked up, and became the usual obsession, before it settled down into a stable relation. Sometimes I wonder why it ever started, this love affair between India and me, and why it has gone on so long. But such moods soon pass, and we settle down into the same old job trot day after day. What shall we do today? What are our plans for tomorrow? Where shall we spend our holidays? And, finally, where shall we retire to?

A love affair between that ocean of humanity, India, and one small atom, not even five and a half feet tall, from a tiny village in Wales? What presumption. Be off with you; choose someone your own size. And yet, I can't think of any other term to describe it. I dream India, eat with her, laugh and cry, rejoice and am sad with her, turn by turn, sometimes all at once. As in every proper love affair, I am as conscious of her shortcomings as she is of mine, and I feel no hesitation in grumbling at her love of finery, her frequent lateness for engagements, or her demands for more money. She in turn very properly grumbles at my superior airs, scoffs at my tall stories, and ridicules my claim to know everything about her. She also keeps a sharp look-out on the slightest tendency for my eyes to stray after any other shapely female form, young or old. Concentrate on my vital statistics, she seems to say, and don't you dare roam around in Spain, or other foreign parts.

I was, of course, lucky in my first contacts and experiences. India led me gently by the hand, drew me into her home, and grappled me to her soul with hooks of steel, forged with a thousand small tendernesses and attentions. From the moment of my arrival, questions buzzed round my mind like a swarm of bees. They were all gravely considered, patiently answered, and lucidly explained. I was instructed in her ways, drawn into her ocean of stories, into her music and poetry, her song and dance, her riotous joys and her ecstatic devotions. I sat through the night at village dramatics, *yatra* parties, or Ramayan *path*. I shared the joint feasts—*ban bhoj*—in the shade of mango trees in blossom at Sunday picnics in the months of Phalgun and Vaisakh. I learned to join with parties singing kirtans, starting quietly and solemnly but before long with hands clapping tempo faster, culminating in a ritual dance. All this was, of course, bit by bit. I did not throw colour for my first two Holis, but soon learned to illuminate my house at Divali, running with the neighbour's children and servants excitedly round the edge of the roof. We put an *akash pradip* on a long pole, burnt many fireworks, and sent a fire balloon into the sky. I accompanied my first *baraat* party with some trepidation, guarding my shoes carefully, wondering what was good manners, whether I would be able to take the late hours, the broad jokes, the food, and, naturally, thinking it was grand after it was all over. I learned to chew the occasional *paan*, to fold my hands in apology if my foot accidentally touched another, and to wash my right hand before food and to rinse the mouth after it. I was taught to bathe from a bucket, sometimes drawn from a well at the crack of dawn on a chilly morning, feeling the water warm as new milk. And, of course, to squat in the privy, though even now I am lost without that essential article, the toilet roll.

LANGUAGE AND LITERATURE

I was helped by a certain facility in language, particularly in what I may call the small change, the *annas* and the *pies* of conversation. My Welsh ear being quick, I caught the lilt and the intonation of Bengali without too much effort, and from there went on to enjoy the village gossip and repartee, the schoolboy jokes, the pithy wisdom of the peasants, the squabbles of the village women and the stories under the stars. From this, later on, came the literature, which underpinned and reinforced what I had picked up through the ear, and so made it my second mother tongue. I think the greatest single thrill of my life was once when, while staying at Santiniketan, Gurudev made me sit on a *mora* beside him, and said, using the 'tumi' of affection, 'From now on speak to me only in Bengali, not even in "khichri bhasa".'

Since coming to live in the skirts of the mountains, my Bengali has become rusty, but it still has a bad influence on my Hindi, mixing my genders all over the place, my vowels all wrong, my grammar and idioms a matter for joking. And my pupils do not spare me in this, as you can well imagine. Still, I get by and am pleased when I am occasionally allowed to teach a Hindi class, in one of the usual 'emergencies' that afflict a school time-table.

What a penance it is to teach from those ill-printed textbooks, and what a joy it is to find more and more finely printed and illustrated books for the young in Hindi and other languages. And how glad I feel when I meet boys in whom I see reflections of my own school days over fifty years ago in a Cheshire village; village boys, suspicious of the town boys and their town-bred ways, get envious of their slick manners and superior talk; determined to get on, to get out of the narrow life of the village (the yearning to get back to it comes much later in life); concentrating on studies, aiming at the 'top' in examination, and sacrificing much of the sweetness and light and fun of life on the way; hampered by lack of books, out-of-date books, out-of-date or indifferent teachers; no one to turn to, when, like a flash from heaven, appears the guru, the teacher who really knows, understands, guides, sympathizes, and rejoices.

Such a teacher I had during my first few years in Bengal, a village Brahmin, who had come to the *zilla* town and worked as a cook while passing sufficient examinations to become a master at the *zilla* school. We read many books together, poetry more than prose, watched many school and village dramatics, spent many holidays taking scouts out in camp, made many excursions to see village *tols* and meet their pandits. He made all the difference to my life in India, bless his soul. I wish every village boy, whether in India or elsewhere, could find one such. I think that part of the miraculous continuity of India through so many misfortunes, so many bad days, during the last five thousand years must be due to the regular flow of such gurus, the 'parampara' from generation to generation of teachers. I would be glad to think that I have been able to join them.

This aspect of life is much better now, I believe, over two generations later than my own school days. That is some consolation. But better for what? Universal pessimism, all round revolt, endless rat races? I have opted out, but still I have to persuade my pupils not to. Their life is still in front of them, and their India is the India of the next fifty or sixty years, as against mine of the last nearly fifty years.

Between us we will cover a century of experience, and what a century! Twenty years of the ending of British rule; nearly a quarter century of Congress rule; and now a quarter century of 'Stri-rajya'! God knows, as one of our political leaders is over-fond of telling us, or 'parkalam', in the words of another, who seems to get by with a lot by simply uttering that one word.

THE CRUCIAL POINT

To come to the crucial point, what does India mean to me today? Before I attempt to answer a question of this nature, caution prompts me to treat it like a shotgun, and fire back with the counter-question: 'Is it loaded?' And a blast from my second barrel: 'Are its terms precise and clear?' Let us assume that the correct answer to my first question is negative, that is, that it is not a loaded question, so go ahead. And indeed the terms of the question, though open to more than one interpretation, are straightforward enough. So what? I am tempted to give a short reply in the classic terms of the bored student to the lecturer who was sermonizing him: 'I cannot hear what you say, sir, because what you are saying is thundering in my ears.' Isn't it obvious, from what I have described, what India means to me today? It is a refuge, a circle of friends, a second birth-place and a home, shining with a familiar face in its mountains, its woods and its fields. It is a civilization that I respect, and a culture that I love.

I am tempted to add an epilogue, what may be termed 'A dip in the Ganges'. As I write this I am sitting high above the river at Hardwar. I have been down to the water's edge at Hari ki Pauri to float a small lamp in its frail boat of leaves and flowers, sending it bobbing and swirling down the swift current, its small light shining bright in the gathering dusk. Near me on the verandah is sitting one of the Hardwar monkeys, peering through the closed grille. He has finished one guava, and is hoping for another; meanwhile he sits quiet, his manners unusually good for a monkey.

The Ganges (sorry, Ganga) flows swift and clear over its stones below, as it has flowed almost since time began, at least since the Himalayas rose up, the glaciers of the last Ice Age started to melt, the snow water cut through the barrier of the Siwaliks, and the sea retreated from the Tethys Gulf. The water laps quietly on the steps at the foot of the house, and I am reminded of the words of an old hymn: 'Time like an ever rolling stream/ Bears all his sons away/ They fly forgotten as a dream/ Dies at the opening day.' Time is still a gipsy man, and nowhere more than by the Ganges, which has borne away the ashes of millions on its broad bosom. Whether it will bear mine I do not know, nor am I greatly concerned, but I do know that I would prefer to be reborn on the soil of India, if there is such a thing as rebirth. This is what India has done to me.

~

ARTHUR HUGHES came to India from Wales in 1927 and lived here for forty-three years, first as a government servant and later as a teacher. He travelled widely during his time in India, spending time in Santiniketan and learning Bengali.

XIV

Those Indian Days

~

PHILLIP KNIGHTLEY

He remembers them all—his racing friends, the mochi who made
his belt, the flavour of the dal his colleague brought him every day.
To him everything in India tastes, smells and feels better ...

K.S.
27 June 1971

I ARRIVED IN INDIA in the same manner—but not the style—
as the Viceroys: by sea. Nine days down the Persian Gulf from
Basorah on the old *Dumra*, travelling second class, getting used
to sleeping in the long hot afternoons and, in the starry-clear
evenings, watching the wake of the ship and wondering where
life was taking me. I had left London after six wasted years
and India was to be but another port of call on the way to
Australia for a personal stock-taking. Then, on 13 December
1960, Bombay—threading our way through the dhows creaking
out for the clove run to East Africa (or the gold run up the
Gulf?) and finally standing outside the customs shed with my
one suitcase, wondering what next!

I had £65(Rs 866 then) in travellers' cheques, 200 Gulf
rupees, ten American dollars and a ticket on the next boat to
Sydney, five months hence. Could I last out? I missed that

boat, and the next. I stayed two years, found a new life, began a new career and later married an Indian girl—thus acquiring at one stroke some 210 Indian relatives. Eight years after I left I still cannot meet an Indian outside India without wanting to talk to him, because I feel sure he will know one of the 550 million whom I know too.

If this sounds emotional, it is because I found India an emotional country. The struggle to exist that is the lot of so many Indians gave me a greater awareness of my own good fortune and deepened my appreciation for the simpler delights of life, while the proximity with death that does not exist in the West (the grey face covered with flowers that passes you when you are on the way home from the cinema) seemed to heighten all feeling from sex to sentimentality.

THE THINGS I DON'T MISS

Trying to grasp the essential difference between my time in India and my time in Europe, I can only come up with this! In India I missed none of the props that now seem such desirable goals in London—a house, a plump bank account, an insurance policy, a portfolio of investments, a television set and a car. It was enough to be alive and well and living in Bombay.

At first I moved in with Roy and Betty Dalgarno in a flat opposite Colaba Post Office and spent a few months in the fantasy world of the Bombay film and racing crowd. (Where are you Omkar Sahib, Bapi Soni and L.P. Rao?) Morning coffee at Gaylords, talking in lakhs when I didn't have hundreds and then a swim with the English jockeys at Breach Candy hoping for a tip that would win me a fortune at Mahalaxmi on Saturday afternoon. It was exciting but unreal, a prolonged holiday that I felt must eventually have a delayed reckoning.

Then, surprisingly, I got a job. A new magazine called *Imprint* was about to start and through Betty Dalgarno I was offered an editorial post: Rs 1200 a month, four weeks' leave, and a return ticket to Australia. By March 1961 I was installed in a flat in Hampton Court, Colaba; I had a German girlfriend, a bearer, liquor permit No.Z04035 entitling me to four units a month, a regular hangover and a bad case of amoebic dysentery (Iraqi, as it turned out).

In the depression following one attack it seemed to me that the real India was slipping away. I was living like a foreigner, and, apart from the different physical surroundings, I might as well have been back in London or Paris. At this stage I met Dr Massa (where are you now, Dr Massa?) and, excepting Betty Dalgarno who remained my guru throughout my stay, he indirectly did more in one consultation to bring me closer to India than anyone else.

Man—and Life—as a Whole

Dr Massa is a spiritual Easterner who, by mistake, was born in the West. He was trained in orthodox Western medicine but tends to practise a blend of allopathy and homoeopathy. He was the first and only doctor I have ever met who treated a patient as a whole human being instead of a collection of symptoms. His prescription for the dysentery was brief: get thinner, you need less food in India than in Europe, so eat sparingly. Don't drink alcohol before meals, and keep up the afternoon nap habit. Then he moved on to the whole human being: 'Everyone needs a consuming interest outside his work.

Find yourself a hobby or a sport, preferably something you can do every day, something you look forward to during working hours. See life as a whole in which work is only a part.'

Mulling this advice over, it seemed to me a recipe for living like an Indian. In general terms Westerners eat and drink too much, take their work too seriously and think sleeping in the afternoon is decadent. In general terms Indians don't eat enough, can always take casual leave if they want to play in a tennis tournament or see a Test match and like to sleep anywhere any time. Since I was in India why not try the Indian way?

NEVER FELT BETTER

So I moved out of my Colaba apartment and took a room with a Parsi family near BEST (Rs 150 a month and a crow that came through the window each morning to wake me up). I ate nothing for breakfast, dal and a chapati or two for lunch, and a light dinner. I bought a motor scooter (I considered a bicycle but everyone said that would be going too far), wore handloom clothes, took up tennis, cut my living allowance to Rs 10 a day and never felt better in my life.

I got my lunch from a colleague at work called Dolly Irani (where are you now, Dolly?) whose grandmother sent her tiffin all the way from Bombay Central. Dolly's grandmother made the best dal in the world: thick, deep yellow, scattered with burnt onion, little patches of ghee glistening on the top, and a flavour that is impossible to describe. No one, and I know my wife will forgive me this, will ever be able to make dal as good as that of Dolly Irani's grandmother.

I got my clothes from Khadi Bhandar. I wandered in one day by accident, discovered *khaddar* and at the same time *chana masala* at two annas a plate (remember this was eight years ago). I chose the material and the Khadi Bhandar tailor made it up for me (where are you now, master?). I still have most of the trousers. The style is sadly dated and the waists seem to have shrunk, but the material and the stitching are still like new.

I joined a tennis club and became a fanatic. Which club to join posed a problem because the wrong choice could have taken me straight back into the world I was in the process of leaving. But the United Services proved ideal. It was (and remains) more Indian than other Bombay club, its service people friendlier and its location magnificent. Also it had a sympathetic tennis marker who judged his fellow men by how they played, not by their status in life (where are you now, Abdul Latif ?). Some of the best Indian friends I had were made through tennis (where are you now Uday Kumar, Lieutenant Singh, Dr Rao, Mr Khatau and Akhtar Ali?).

Getting to Know People

I took more interest in my office colleagues. Why had Mr Khatri chosen accountancy? Where had Devidas Gawaskar learned to draw? What was life like for Sheila Trace in the YWCA? Soon I knew more Indians than Europeans. Apart from friends, I knew on chatting terms people like the man in Pasta Lane who fixed my punctures, the man in Sassoon Dock who welded my broken lamp bracket, the man at the studio who developed my film, the *mochi* outside Liberty Cinema who made my belts, the *bhuttawala* at Dhobi Talao, the juice squeezer on Colaba Causeway, the owner of the lassi shop opposite Blitz, the *jamadar* who cleaned the office...

I investigated not only regional Indian cooking (and distilling) but also the best Anglo-Indian dishes, an unfairly demeaned cuisine that will one day be better appreciated: chilli fry, country captain, potato chop, prawn cutlets, mutton stew.

I queued for hours to take my scooter riding test. I spent a whole day in the docks to clear a parcel from Australia. I visited the magistrate's courts, wrote to the newspapers, had a row with Frank Moraes over the role of the press in India and was caught in a Prohibition raid on a private party (the man in a dhoti on whom I had been pressing drinks turned out to be an inspector in the Anti-Corruption Squad).

I began writing film scripts, first for Durga Khote Productions and then for the Government of India Films Division: how to understand metric weights, why the farmers should use fertilizer and then in that traumatic month in November 1962, 'give your blood for the jawans on the Indo-Chinese frontier'. I began to feel Indian, aggressively defensive over the liberation of Goa, fiercely patriotic over the border trouble with China and patronizingly tolerant of the first tourists, twenty-one-day birds of package who would never know the real India.

In September 1962, I accepted an assignment from Durga Khote to make a film in Delhi for the 2nd Punjab Regiment, Brigade of Guards, the oldest regiment in the Indian army, which was celebrating its 200th anniversary. I moved into the lines at Rashtrapati Bhavan, commuted daily to the Red Fort with the camera team, helped by the young Sikh in charge of the motor pool (where are you now, Captain P.P. Singh?) and the dashing officer from UP who was organizing the film.

It was a fortnight of rehearsals and drill, interspersed with sightseeing, tennis and an endless round of parties, sitar recitals, films and, like everywhere in India, conversation (I talked more in India in a night than I do in a month in London). Then the presentation of colours, the ball with more beautiful women in one place than anywhere in the world, the JCO's dinner with a table creaking under silver collected over two centuries, and—could I have imagined it?—a young Sikh captain steadily munching his way around the rim of a champagne glass until only the stem was left. 'Take no notice of him,' someone said. 'He does it at every party.'

From Delhi I took the third class sleeper to Pathankot and then a bus to Srinagar. The road had been washed away and the journey took two days. At lunch on the second day at some tiny roadside hotel, the south Indian couple at my table found that the waiter, not surprisingly, spoke no Tamil and no English. They, on the other hand, spoke no Hindi. I surprised myself by interpreting for them and in a sudden flush of confidence began speaking Hindi right and left, getting involved in complicated conversation with complete strangers and leaving them bewildered.

IDENTIFY YOURSELF

My finest moment came when the postmaster at Srinagar told me in English that he could not pay me a money order from Bombay unless I could produce someone from Srinagar who knew me well and I was able to tell him in Hindi that if I knew someone in Srinagar well then I would have taken money from him and not from Bombay. (At least that's what

I intended to say.) Anyway, he paid up.

I spent a week snowed up in Gulmarg, longing for the plains, then took the train back to Bombay. I remember very well that the ticket cost me Rs 56 and thinking that if I saved furiously for a while I could spend the rest of my life on the road, as the hippies say, travelling on the railways of India, eating toast dribbling with butter and drinking endless cups of that incomparable railway tea.

From Bombay I took a boat to Goa, sleeping on the deck with my bedding-roll that I now carried with me everywhere. My memories of Goa are vague except for a magnificent crab curry, tiny little soft-shelled crabs on brown rice that the grain store in Bombay referred to contemptuously as 'servant's' rice and which in London I now buy at a health food store and pay double for it because it is grown 'macrobiotically'.

It is now obvious that my memories of India are mingled inextricably with taste sensations, but this only goes to confirm my earlier theory that everything in India tastes, smells and feels better because with the Indian way of life the senses are more alive. It is all in danger, of course. Now everyone seems to want to join the Western rush for consumer durables. The pace of life is speeding up. (Whatever happened to those taxi drivers you had to beg to hurry?) The advertising men are taking over. Indians, like the West, are discovering wants they never knew existed.

Yet surely it is more civilized to have an institution called 'casual leave' than for everyone to have a high-fidelity radiogram? (If economists are to be believed, if you want the one you have to sacrifice the other.) And television is on the way. This will certainly spell the end to that social ease that is India's great attraction. No more dropping in unannounced, no more spontaneous parties, no more all-night conversations. Once the square-eyed monster moves in he rules absolutely.

Still, no matter what happens, no one can change the India of 1960–62. I remember the time slipping easily by, the years turning over with that soothing certainty peculiar to a calendar marked by religious festivals. Every day seemed a joy, every night held the promise of romantic adventure. I would play tennis until nearly dark, watch the sun set over the Arabian Sea and ride back from Colaba Point along a road lined with freshly bathed people out for their evening walk, sniffing smoke from the wood fires, and watching the lights blink on along the verandah of the Navy Hospital. The rest of the world was going mad, the Cuban missile crisis threatening everyone with oblivion, but the India I knew was there for ever.

~

PHILLIP KNIGHTLEY was a journalist with the *Daily Telegraph* and the foreign correspondent for the *Daily Mirror*. He came to India in 1960, married an Indian woman and was managing editor of the Bombay literary magazine *Imprint*. He has written several books on war and espionage including *The First Casualty* and *The Second Oldest Profession*, as well as his autobiography, *A Hack's Progress*.

XV

From Revolt to Love

~

MAURICE ZINKIN

*He came to India as a gesture of revolt against parental authority.
In his mind were Romance and Kipling. What he found was hard
work, many friends, continuing education. He ended up with a
tremendous love and respect for the country.*

K.S.

18 February 1971

I WENT TO THE Indian Civil Service by accident, as a gesture
of adolescent revolt.

When I went up to Cambridge in 1932, I knew nothing of
India. None of the family had ever been out of Europe, except
for an uncle in the United States. I had never been abroad,
except once to Belgium. We had only done English and European
history at school. I had heard of Clive and Plassey, but never
of Wellesley and Assaye, of the Nana Saheb but never of
Curzon. Even the great Civil Disobedience movement of 1931
had made very little impact on my mind; in so far as I
thought of public affairs at all, it was of the unemployment
of my native North, of the view as one came down from the
moors into Oldham, with its forest of cotton-mill chimneys,
and only two still smoking.

ROMANCE

At first I was not very bothered about careers. My mother
wanted me to be a barrister, and that did not appeal to me.
I was attracted for a moment by the army, but my mother
thought that was unsuitable for someone so heavily intellectual,
and she was probably right. Then, some time in my second
year I think, Manzur Qadir was having tea in my rooms one
day, and suddenly asked me why I did not think of the ICS.
I knew nothing about the ICS except what I had read in
Kipling, and Kipling is much more about Jat peasants and
private soldiers than he is about Collectors or Secretaries to
the government. Indeed, one gets the impression that he
rather disliked the Service.

As Manzur talked, however, he stirred again the romantic
vein Kipling had already touched. *Kim, The Jungle Book* and
Plain Tales from the Hills had been amongst my favourite books
as a boy. They ranked with P.G. Wodehouse and Jane Austen.
From them I had got the feeling that Indians were immensely
likable people. I had admired the courage of Hurree Chunder
Mookerjee, and the devotion to duty of the Gurkhas at the
lying-in-state of Edward VII, and the saintliness of the Lama.
I had not realized that the Lama was Tibetan and different;
nor had I realized how heavily Kipling's stories were
concentrated on the North-West, and especially the Punjab.

Manzur drew me a picture of a life of worthwhile work.
The ICS, as he described it, existed to keep order and to do
justice, to develop the country and to be impartial amongst
its interest groups. He did not pretend it was an easy life.
There was a lot to do, the climate was hot and district towns
did not have every modern amenity. But clearly it was a job

where one could do good, and exercise responsibility, and have position and power as well. I was attracted. I did not even ask him why, though he was the son of a High Court judge (and later to be Foreign Minister of Pakistan), he had not considered the Service himself.

I went home and told my mother about this new idea. She exploded. She liked my Indian friends, and especially Manzur. She found their manners charming, and she approved strongly of their respect for their parents. But India was associated in her mind with tigers and she did not consider me capable of coping with tigers. Above all, India was 5600 miles away, and she wanted her sons to have careers where they could come and see her every week.

Perhaps ordinarily I would have listened. She was a widow, and had some right to her sons' company. But somehow at that moment she touched my burgeoning sense of independence. I was eighteen, and thought that I had the right to decide for myself what career I should follow. The more she argued, the more determined I grew. From then on, I never considered any other possibility but the ICS. I put my name down for the Home Civil Service as well, in order to please my mother, and got in, but I never dreamed of taking it. Business I did not so much as consider, though even then one would have done better financially in big business than in the Service.

When I arrived in India in 1938 I still did not know much about the country. I had put my name down for the Bombay Presidency because I laboured under the illusion that Bangalore and Ootacamund were in Bombay. I had learnt some Marathi, some Indian law and a great deal of Indian history—I was a historian by training, and so found the history fascinating. It helped considerably too in enabling me to pass at the top of my class.

And Reality

I was sent first to Sholapur. It was just after the end of the monsoon, and soon after I arrived, I was sent out on tour with the Assistant Collector to whom I was attached. I enjoyed all the usual things, the ride to the village in the cool of the morning, the chats with the villagers about their troubles, the nights under the stars, the friendliness of the other people in the station when one came in from tour. There were less than a dozen couples in the Club, but they all went out of their way to make a rather homesick youngster feel at home. I was asked endlessly to dinner, and above all I was talked to for hours at a time about India. In those first few months I was indoctrinated into the ways and attitudes of official society, and above all into the all-pervadingness of work. Work filled the day, and 'shop' (or gossip) the evenings. For getting the feel of a new life, the gossip was as useful as the 'shop', for nothing reveals the values of a small society as quickly as its gossip. Some of the people were rather limited, some, by the standards of 1971, rather snobbish. But all of them minded about doing their jobs thoroughly and uprightly; and all of them, from the Collector to the bank manager, believed that their doing these jobs properly was important to the welfare of India.

Politics Bug

In retrospect, however, the person who affected me most was not anybody at the Club, but the revenue clerk who taught me Marathi. He was a Deshastha Brahmin, whose father was a Deputy Collector and who was himself to rise to be a Collector. Like so many Maharashtrian Brahmins, he was a man of the most total integrity; he gave me a respect for the Maharashtrian character which has never left me. He was also a passionate nationalist, and we spent far more time arguing about Indian Independence than we did on Marathi. My Marathi never became very good; but I acquired a passion for Indian politics which has taken up a great deal of my time ever since, and which to this day makes me spend many a happy weekend reading books and articles on Congress Party organization, or the effect of caste and faction on voting in west UP, or the connection between Ezhavas and communism in Kerala.

I have never been able to summon up an equal interest in English politics, though the incompetence of Harold Wilson did move me to a certain passion. The only time in my life when I have felt like joining in a riot, was when Nehru tried to separate Bombay city from Maharashtra; I was restrained only by the vague feeling that it would be a slightly ridiculous way for a middle-aged Englishman to behave. In India I used to talk politics ten or fifteen hours a week, and we still spend whole evenings doing so when Indian friends come to visit. I do not suppose I spend more than an hour a week talking English politics. In England it is the economy one talks about; and one does that less and less as one has discovered how unresponsive it is to all one's favourite remedies.

Indian politics were worth discussing. The confrontation between the British and the Congress and the Muslim League was one of the great political confrontations of all time, even if to an extraordinary degree the contestants were always talking past each other.

It seemed to me then, and it still seems to me now, that the whole difficulty was that there was something in what everybody was saying.

My official seniors were right in stressing that law and order does not just happen; it has to be worked for day and night, it is always fragile—one could go for miles in the countryside without seeing a policeman—and it is terribly dependent on the prestige of the government and the people's belief in its willingness to react decisively to disorder. The gossip included endless stories about how riots had been averted by a jest, or a display of firmness at the right time or even a well-chosen threat to the man behind the trouble; but though the stories were told lightly enough, there always lurked behind them the reminder of how easily and irretrievably the situation could have gone wrong. Some of the stories indeed were about the occasions when it did go wrong; in my very first year we had a nasty riot in Sholapur, which revealed to me, as so many other riots have done since, how helpless the authorities are against the quick stab in a back-alley, with no other motive but a difference of religion. In Delhi in 1947, a man was killed by a stab in the back in front of me; I saw him die, but I never saw the murderer.

Self-rule's the Best

My Marathi teacher and my Indian ICS contemporaries were equally right when they argued that good government was no substitute for self-government, that the reforms which were needed could not come from foreigners, and that the society was less splintered into groups, more of a nation than most of my elders believed. The British official hated moneylenders and untouchability probably more than the Congress politicians did; but his capacity to do something about them was much less. What we admired most about the Congress government of 1937–39 was its legislation protecting the peasant; and we were bound to sympathize with their efforts against untouchability. I remember, in 1940 one of my *mamlatdars* refusing to take tea with me. He was a delightful and courteous old gentleman, but his reason was that to do so would pollute him. When I was once invited into a Hindu temple in my jurisdiction, and duly made my offering to Lord Krishna like anybody else, there was a debate in the municipality about the outrage, and the temple had, I understand, to be purified.

Then there were the Muslims, especially my bearer, who were always impressing upon me their distrust of the Hindus. They were very conscious of their different religious traditions, and they had a totally exaggerated view of their past glories, but above all they had a perfectly straightforward fear of being a minority, and therefore discriminated against. To me, this seemed a perfectly reasonable fear, for the Europe from which I came was full of discrimination. Across the water in Ireland there was plenty of it, and yet Catholic and Protestant Irishmen were just as much all Irish to me as Muslims and Hindus were both Indians.

Most interesting of all were the loyalists, especially the junior officials. They took an instrumental view of the British. They found us useful because they trusted our impartiality. I do not think that they thought us any better than anybody else; but we did have the advantage that our caste fellows and our school friends and our cousins were six thousand miles away.

From Sholapur I went to West Khandesh. All the senior officials were Indian, the only other Englishman was the Assistant Superintendent of Police. In West Khandesh, therefore, I had my first real taste of the enormous warmth of Indian society, the endless willingness to help and explain and put oneself out, the permanence of friendship.

Amongst the rather limited number of gurus I have had, Hari Singh, the Forest Officer, Purviz Damry, the Special Officer for Bhil Uplift, and V. Isvaran, the Collector, rank very high. They taught me to administer, than which no job is more satisfying; and they showed me how to detect the innumerable traps which lie in wait for any carelessness of those who have power. Not to take bribes is easy; to be alert to flattery, to hold the balance equal between people one liked and people one does not, to say 'no' when saying 'no' is unpleasant, these take learning.

I learnt from them too to see work as central to life. West Khandesh was lonely; when one went on tour one had nobody to relax with for a month at a time. It was physically uncomfortable and I had malaria every month. But it was work worth doing. Jarilla cotton was just being introduced to the Khandesh peasant. We were trying to improve the local poultry. Above all, we were running a great campaign to protect the Bhils from the depredations of their moneylenders, who were amongst the worst in India, I suppose partly because the Bhil was a somewhat unsatisfactory debtor.

One remembers other things too: the pleasure of the little village girls when they got a ride in the car if they promised to go to school; endless lectures to, I suspect, totally unconvinced villagers on the merits of compost-pits and the

evils of bride payments and cradles which did not keep the
baby's back straight; the joys of long morning rides and the
jungle at night. We all worked twelve and fourteen hours a
day—I once got an official reproof from my Collector for
trying cases until ten o'clock at night. But we could see the
results of our work, we could feel the people were the better
for our efforts, and that made everything worthwhile, even
the difficult moments when one had to make decisions which
might prove costly for one's career, alone, without anybody
to ask for advice. West Khandesh was a good place to learn
to stand on one's own feet.

EDUCATION CONTINUES

It was in West Khandesh, too, that I learnt to have a respect
for at least some local politicians which is today unfashionable.
We had in Kandirbar a lawyer called Shah. He was a moderate
lawyer, but a very good Congressman. He combined a
proper deference to one as the magistrate in court with
straightforwardly firm nationalist views. He was the sort of
man who, if he had become a backbench MLA would perhaps
have been willing to lobby for a school for a village which had
voted for him; but no more than that. He was a profoundly
decent human being. I suppose the left-wing intellectual would
despise him as conservative, orthodox and too concerned with
his clients. But to me it is men like him, more than the great
national leaders, who made the Congress so special amongst
the political parties of Asia.

From West Khandesh I went on to the secretariat, first in
Bombay and then in Delhi, and in due course into business.
But already in those first three years, the essential lessons had

been learned. The moment when one leaves university and goes out into the world is (or at least was in those days) the most formative in a man's life. One has to learn to work, even when the work is routine, to cooperate with people, even when one does not like them particularly, to take responsibility and stand up for one's ideas of what is right, even if it might be expensive. At the university, it is easy to have ideals. When one goes to work, one has to find out how much of them can be carried out, how quickly, and by what means.

For all of this there is nothing to equal an Indian district. In the old phrase, it makes boys into men. It certainly did that for me. It does more. It gives one friends, and standards with which to understand one's friends. Today, after nearly thirty years, and in very different circumstances, much of my life is still governed by the rules I learned in the district. Many of my dearest friends still go back to those early years of my service.

One did not of course petrify in 1941. I went on deepening my understanding of the traditions of my service; I am still, I hope, learning from men like A.B. Gorwala and H.M. Patel. Burra Venkatappiah was to give me an understanding of what karma means to the Hindu, which has greatly influenced me. I came to appreciate the true Brahmin austerity of men like Professors Gadgil, Karve and Dandekar. In all my time in India, I was always learning, always being warmed by the affection of new and old friends. But what essentially India gave me, I was given at the very beginning. For it was then that I was taught the importance of doing a job properly, that I acquired the intellectual excitement of an interest in Indian politics and anthropology and history, and that I really learned to respond to the warmth Indians reserve for their friends.

~

MAURICE ZINKIN entered the Indian Civil Service in 1938. He began as a supernumerary Assistant Collector, touring the remote tribal lands of the Bhils on horseback, collecting revenue and enforcing law and order. He worked for Unilever in India between 1949 and 1960, later becoming sales director of Lever Brothers. He was a noted writer and during the 1950s, he published two books on development economics: *Asia and the West* (1950) and *Development for Free Asia* (1956). He died in 2002.

XVI

More Gallimaufry

~

C.R. MANDY

'DEAR INDIA!' SAID THE erstwhile memsahib in the bar of the London Hilton. 'Wasn't it lovely signing chits for all those drinks? It did not matter if you had any money or not.'

You see it all depends on the way you look at it!

I find my time in India difficult to assess, as the three periods into which my stay was divided were utterly different though each in retrospect is, to me, memorable and delightful. The first period consisted of a spell in the former Kathiawar at a Griassia Chiefs' college, the second as an Indian army Major, the third as an editor in Bombay.

The Kathiawar days brought me in touch with a world that no longer exists; a fantastic, feudal world of princes, *talukdars* of every description. They were, for the most part, very backward individuals who lived in medieval walled towns and in ornate, rather repulsive palaces with façades resembling a stale, off-colour wedding cake. Shikar was their main interest and I was soon initiated into every aspect of the game and learnt to distinguish between mallard, pochard, teal and the untouchable coot. There were great ceremonial partridge, sandgrouse and quail shoots, and I became familiar with the pursuit of floricon and cunj on the Rann of Cutch. Less attractive was the chase after chinkara and nilgai deer from fast cars in the same area. I made a nodding acquaintance with the scraggy lions in the scraggy Gir forest. And there was one maharaja who provided entertainment for his guests by dynamiting crocodiles; the unfortunate magar would eventually surface like a damaged submarine, blood pouring from its mouth. Elsewhere, a goat was tied up for one's delectation, and one awaited the coming at midnight of an esurient panther.

MEDIEVAL SPLENDOURS

Amid this medieval milieu there were aesthetic delights such as the russet-tinted Gir Mar at sunset in Junagadh, the premier state where the Nawab found ritualistic satisfaction in dogs' weddings. And I remember with awe the trek to the wonderful, temple-crowned hill at Palitana. The names come back over the dusty years—Junagadh, Gondal, Jamnagar, Morvi, Porbandar, Dhrangadhra, Bhavnagar; and with them a phalanx of quaint characters. There was the lesser raja whose interests never rose above domestic pets and who, when Lady Willingdon asked him where the rani was, apologetically explained that she was not present because she was not 'house-trained'. Then there was the senile, opium-sated raja who was able to recite by heart much of Goldsmith's 'Deserted Village', and my friend, the *durbar sahib*, in the lapel of whose ancient, food-stained coat, a pair of cockroaches lived happily, and the surgically minded, but medically unqualified yuvaraj who invited me to his palace to see him perform a major operation on one of his subjects.

There were bad lads among these medieval potentates and

I overheard much inside gossip about them when I visited the British sahibs in the Kathiawar territory. The raja of X had poisoned one of his concubines with kurrum, a poison derived from the oleander bush (I have looked askance at oleander ever since those days!). The raja of Y had pushed his dewan over a cliff into the Indian Ocean (which seemed to me an admirable way of getting rid of recalcitrant chief ministers!). To my youthful eyes, Kathiawar in the 1930s was a Jabberwockian land. The 'gun-salute rulers' and their 'durbaris' were as resplendent as nobles in England in the days of the Tudors. There were benevolent, paternalistic despots among them, but the majority could be described as hedonistic drones, and their passing is certainly a matter of little regret. My experience of them was a strange, unorthodox introduction to India. They belonged to the mind of Edward Lear, and perhaps their most percipient and amusing laureates have been E.M. Forster (*The Hill of Devi*) and J.R. Ackerley (*Hindoo Holiday*).

Kathiawar meant much to me. I was young and its brisk, healthy, sparkling winter mornings, with the vocal *cunj* flying in arrow formation above my bungalow, were indeed very heaven.

KHAKI INTELLIGENCE

The shift to GHQ, New Delhi, in the war years resembled an entry into still another world. I knew the city superficially, in transit to Kashmir and Kulu. I arrived as a Captain (attached to the 10th Baluchi regiment) and found myself posted to an Intelligence Unit in the north block at GHQ. It was the height of the hot season, with the *loo* wind and a violent dust-storm blowing. I felt forlorn and bewildered in this heart of darkness. The section's Mess in Aurangzeb Road was like an oven. It was to be my home for nearly two years until Lord Louis Mountbatten transferred his SEAC headquarters to the greenery of Kandy in Ceylon.

'The first thing you must acquire is a bicycle,' the Mess secretary informed me helpfully. So I bought a second-hand machine in Connaught Circus. Later, in the winter mornings, it was bitterly cold, cycling up to GHQ, and at night returning from an Intelligence Unit in the Red Fort. I hesitated for some time to wear gloves, until I passed a beefy, cycling British Brigadier wearing them, and gladly followed suit. I tended to get lost after dark in the roundabouts and avenues of New Delhi. 'You must steer by the stars,' the Mess secretary was helpful once more.

Work in the Intelligence Unit in the North Block was interesting. Because I spoke Siamese, I earned a promotion and was allocated to the Siamese section. I had known the Major in charge during my early days in Bangkok when he sold soap for Levers. He was now a big boss and inclined to mild bull-shittery ('Captain Mandy, the waste-paper basket is not the place for top secret documents'), but our Colonel still referred to him as old Soapy so and so. It was the period when the Arakan campaign was in full swing, and one of my initial duties was to pinpoint positions at the morning session in the Map Room. This entailed an all-night vigil with a Corporal from the cipher section as assistant. I had undergone a brief course in cartography but was still fairly dumb at the job and increasingly apprehensive as the signals in code from the Arakan piled up.

After some weeks a fellow Captain who was equally dumb at the task, made havoc ('a right balls-up,' the Colonel called

it) with his pin-pointing, and there was consternation and
horror in the Map Room next morning in the presence of
Wingate, Auchinleck and other top brass. As a result, only
senior officers were to be given the job and I was much
relieved to be relieved of the intricate niceties of latitude and
longitude.

There were numerous alphabetical categories in our
Intelligence Unit. I asked an officer in department Z what his
duties were, and he replied nonchalantly, 'We arrange
assassinations.' Another officer in B section was busily engaged
in composing anti-Japanese slogans in Siamese on matchboxes
to be dropped as propaganda over the paddy fields around
Bangkok. Reports from secret agents and contracts came in
from the Siamese underground movement in a swelling flood.
In addition, we had to interrogate Siamese-speaking captives
in the Red Fort, and there was an occasional top secret visit
to Bombay or Karachi to contact and pump (no alcoholic
expenses spared) neutral escapees from Siam.

In my recreation time, I got to know Delhi as I had not
experienced it before—the Lodi tombs, Hauz Khas, the
alleyways of Old Delhi, the Roshanara Club. It is a city
which, since then, has always entranced me. On moonlit nights
at the Aurangzeb Mess, one could lie snugly in bed and listen
to the jackals as they raucously came down to the avenues
from the Ridge.

New Friends

The Mess was a self-contained world, almost hermetically
sealed off from outside. The officers drank morosely and
incessantly played liar dice. They had no Indian friends nor any

real contact with Indian life. I was lucky in knowing an English couple in Tughlak Road who were interested in Indian art and writing. At their house I met Ahmed Ali, the author of *Twilight in Delhi*, and some of Jamini Roy's family. We would foregather on Sunday evenings, along with a remarkable Chinese scholar who worked under me as a Flight Lieutenant in our Siamese section—Harold Acton, and who had been for a number of years in Peking University. My first meeting with Acton took place in the North Block. One of my areas for intelligence purposes was Yunnan, apparently because it was contiguous to North Siam. I found the names and movements of Chiang Kai-shek's Generals in Yunnan a proper headache and asked my Colonel if he could procure for me a fluent Chinese speaker to help me out. Nothing happened for several months, until one day, the colonel rang up to say, 'I've got your man and am sending him up for vetting.' He did not mention any name. Some minutes later, a bald, bespectacled, benign individual in a Flight Lieutenant's uniform arrived at my desk. He said he spoke Mandarin and had been in Peking.

'Ah,' I said, 'I've just read an enjoyable novel about Peking— *Peonies and Ponies* by Harold Acton. Have you ever met him?'

'I am Harold Acton,' said the Flight Lieutenant, with a smile. Harold Acton and I explored the artistic life of Delhi in the following months, a most pleasurable interlude in army life. At that time there was not in the city the lively nucleus of outstanding Indian artists and authors which I was to encounter later in the 1950s, when I was to meet writers Ruth Prawer Jhabvala, Nirad Chaudhuri, Sardar Khushwant Singh, the artist Krishen Khanna, and other notable painters, in residence there.

Meanwhile at the GHQ, life was increasingly hectic. The Japanese thrust had been stemmed at Kohima and Imphal, and to some extent the initiative was passing to Mountbatten's forces. The Supremo, frustrated by the deviation of his supplies and landing craft to the Anzio landings in Italy, and by the static attitude of Chiang Kai-shek, decided to postpone the sea assault on Rangoon, and moved his SEAC headquarters to Ceylon, and my next two years were spent in Kandy, Siam and Malaya.

The Editorial We

I returned to India for my third period in 1946, the beginning of a twelve-year sojourn at the *Illustrated Weekly Of India*. I was no stranger to Bombay and relished the prospect of living in this vital, beautiful, cosmopolitan city.

In an editorial chair, one is progressively educated as one absorbs knowledge every moment of the day. This was brought home to me when my secretary, on one occasion, informed me that there was a gentleman outside the office door, in a militant mood, with a poised umbrella! He had taken umbrage about a feature on the X community. I was able to placate my visitor and at the same time learnt much about the community in question, which was all grist to the editorial mill. I travelled extensively through all parts of India in these years and made deep and lasting friendships with folks of all communities. Many of these friends consisted of journalists, writers, artists and actors—the four categories of people with whom I feel most at ease anywhere in the world. It was necessary for me, in the course of my work sometimes to meet politicians, and I encountered some splendid persons among them, such as

Rafi Ahmed Kidwai and Jayaprakash Narayan, but, on the whole, I find myself in agreement with that brilliant, coat-trailing iconoclast Nirad Chaudhuri, when he speaks of the faces of certain Indian politicians as 'swollen with pride and arrogance and disfigured by a wily cynicism'. (Is America any different?) Nirad Chaudhuri goes on to assert that gatherings of Indian politicians resemble 'rows of dirty linen bundles in a dhobi's godown'. A Gaelic proverb puts the matter less truculently and more mellifluously: 'One cannot find the voice of love in the ministry of finance'. A bad politician in any country is surely an individual who manipulates the self-interest of other men to put himself in a position where he can concentrate on his own. The estimable politician in India should, of course, be a campaigner who sallies forth earnestly into the mofussil to teach backward peasants how to increase the fertility of their fields and reduce that of their womenfolk.

PEOPLE, PEOPLE

But I fear that Mr Chaudhuri's unprepossessing, nepotistic 'types' are commonplace sights. I heard much of corruption in Indian government circles but the evildoers seemed to me positively amateurish when compared with the politicians in Ceylon! Once, on holiday in Kashmir, I met a prominent Bengali politician with a very bad reputation indeed. 'He would steal candy from a child,' an American diplomat told me. We were staying at Nedou's Hotel and the Bengali politician had a big brood of children, all of whom would troop in after him obediently for the midday meal, like a gaggle of happy geese. He was obese and jovial and beamed radiantly on this well-behaved, gradated family. If he was a crook, he was the most domesticated, jolly crook I have ever seen! I said so to the American diplomat later. 'Ah,' he said succinctly, 'one can smile and smile and be a villain!'

One of the most delightful persons I ever met in India was Sarojini Naidu. I once took a staff photographer to do an interview with her. She bubbled with wit and joie de vivre. Shakespeare, or at least one of the Restoration dramatists, could have used her advantageously as a simpatico character of note. When she was posing, she said to my cockney staff photographer, 'Place me carefully, good man. Sometimes I look like a genial frog.'

Breakfast with Pandit Nehru in February 1959 was another memorable occasion. I did not analyse him in depth over the meal, as Dom Moraes and Ved Mehta have done, but I was impressed by his human side when he took me afterwards to see his pandas in their quarters in the garden, where he donned gloves and fed the animals with dates.

The Mahatma I saw only once—at Itarsi junction. Kasturba was massaging him in a third class carriage, with a crowd waiting for *darshan* on the platform. As I watched him fascinated, my pocket was adroitly picked!

Of course there was a colour bar in India, just as there is in England (though the British try to deny it). The Punjabis despised the southerners for their dark countenances and the latter, to judge from the stress on the 'wheaten complexions' of potential brides in the matrimonial advertisements in the *Hindu*, were envious of the pink faces of the northerners. I personally found northerners good company, as I have found Madrasis; but for conversation and coruscating argument, the Bengali intellectual was the best company of all. I fancy, I subconsciously sensed that there was an element of Irishry in their volatility, and of the Far East in their visages, which compelled me to respond readily to them.

STARGAZING

As the nominal editor of *Filmfare*, I came into contact with a galaxy of film stars, such impressive and immensely affable personalities as Prithviraj, Dilip Kumar and Raj Kapoor, and, among the women, with numerous talented and overwhelmingly beautiful people. But, alas, they were too often scriptless and almost directorless (except for Satyajit Ray). I can still visualize Ashok Kumar and Devika Rani and, though so long ago, yet recall the tune of that haunting song from *Acchut Kanya*. And what pleasure I derived from Indian dancing—the superb Balasaraswati, Shanta Rao, Sitara, and many others.

One of my criticisms of India, and I put it forth humbly, is that the second-rater too frequently gets to the top. I knew a worthy but talentless professor in a responsible position who appeared to think that 'out of sight, out of mind' meant 'invisible and insane'. He once asked me, in all seriousness, why the English always referred to summery instead of to wintry justice! Some of these characters rose in life because they had gone to jail during the swaraj movement and deserved to be rewarded. I was reminded of this in Ireland last year when I heard a story of a man whose wife got into difficulties while swimming off the Wicklow shore. He called urgently to the beach guard, who said he could not swim.

'How in heaven did you get the job then?' asked the anxious husband.

'Because, sorr, I was the only candidate who had been to prison, in the troubled times, for my political convictions,' answered the guard.

I recollect nostalgically, the abundant loveliness of India— apple-scented evenings in the exquisite Kulu valley, the temples of Mahabalipuram at dusk, looking upon 'faerie seas forlorn', the pewter glimmer of the mermaid-invoking beaches of Kovallam and Calangute, the snows of Kanchenjunga and Sinniolahu from Darjeeling, the blue Nilgiris, Benares and Jaisalmer, Udaipur and Mandu ... a catalogue of enchantment, etched in memory and unfadable.

There was, on the other hand, the dark side, the Louis Malle image—the poverty of Calcutta, the cobweb-laden chawls of Bombay, and squalid Kamatipura to which the American senator, the late Estes Kefauver requested that I should take him. (Prostitution, he felt, could be hygienicized and even glamorized, as the Japanese years ago dealt with it in their rigorously inspected, decoratively clean yoshiwaras at Kobe and Yokohama). Such grim conditions and degradation are, however, not peculiar to India, as some Western journalists would insist. I have seen the equivalent in Naples, Barcelona, Marrakesh, and in the still unpoliced, Jack-the-Ripper areas of the East End of London, where I would not venture to walk at night.

An aspect of India which has greatly impressed me and filled me with admiration is its secularism. I have met Muslim envoys representing India in London, Washington, Cairo, Bonn and Rangoon—all men of prime capacity, chosen for their abilities, with no stipulation where religion is concerned. I still have a diminishing number of friends (now Pakistanis) from the days of the Raj and I cannot help thinking of them as Indians in essence. The creation of Pakistan is to me the major blunder of this infelicitous century. And the Raj? At its best, I reckon, it produced self-denying men of integrity (as it never did in Ireland, from Cromwellian times to the Easter rebellion of 1916). Some of these officials loved India to their deepest instincts; tyrants like General Dyer were the exception rather than the rule and he, in his way, had his grim usefulness in that Jallianwala Bagh was a turning point in history.

I shall revisit India, and I shall be going again, I hope, to old friends and fondly remembered places. I shall, however, have to do so without undue delay, as I have reached the age when, to quote Ezra Pound:

'The days are not full enough
And the nights are not full enough
And life slips by like a field mouse
Not shaking the grass.'

~

C.R. MANDY served as a major in the Indian army during the Second World War. In 1946 he joined the *Illustrated Weekly of India* as its editor and stayed on for twelve years. In his capacity as editor of the *Weekly* and nominal editor of *Filmfare* he met many prominent leaders and celebrities of the time.

XVII

A Changing Scene

~

RAWLE KNOX

AT NO TIME IN my youth did I think of going to India. It seemed quite enough to know all about the place. For, of course, I could tell anyone about the population and the history and the religions and the geography of India, and about the Congress movement too. We were all socialists then and India was a popular subject for debate. Arthur Lall was at Balliol with me, but I think I can be excused for seeing him plain as a table tennis wizard, rather than anticipating that he would in the future represent a sometime free India in an unborn United Nations.

THOSE PALMY DAYS!

By the middle 1930s, when I went down from Oxford, the clouds over Europe were thick enough to obscure any further vision. Mussolini's invasions of Abyssinia and Albania, the Spanish civil war, the rise of Hitler and the shame (as I saw it) of Munich were political issues that pervaded one's work and even one's private life. They were so vivid to a European in his twenties that other pictures went unseen in shadowed corners. Even the liberal British mind related the prospect of

Indian independence to the necessities of war against Nazi Germany and her allies.

I was brought up in the kind of way that made Poona and 'pucca' automatic joke words when spoken on the music hall stage. Yet, my great-grandfather Knox had been a chaplain to the East India Company in the Madras Presidency and his elder brother, Sir George Knox, had risen to be Senior Puisne Judge of the Allahabad High Court. My Knox grandfather married the daughter of Bishop French of Lahore and had several cousins (I remember them standing around aloofly at his funeral) who rose to high positions in the Indian Army.

None of these connections registered with me when I was young, and I have only become interested in them since. So that India was to me still a strange distant area of undefined light when I found myself, as a result of enlisting in the war against Hitler, aboard a troopship at Greenock, Scotland, and bound for Bombay. It was New Year's Day, 1941. In 1855 my great-grandfather, at the age of eighteen, had departed from India and spent three months, between January and April, sailing home. I was about to spend the same period, in wartime conditions, on my way to renew the Knox family's acquaintance with India.

At Bombay, a sort of postings lottery took place aboard ship, and after the draw I was ordered to the Mountain Artillery Training Centre at Ambala to await transfer to the 22nd Mountain Regiment, IA, then serving in Malaya. Just about all I remember of the tràin journey is the *pankahwallah* lying on his back on the platform and operating the resturant *pankah* by means of a string attached to his big toe and leading through a hole in the wall. Really, that seems a hell of a long time ago.

At Ambala I made my first contact with the active military since leaving the south coast of England where we had been frantically preparing the alleged defences against an imminently expected German invasion. I found regular Indian Army officers seething with wrath against the new C-in-C, General Auchinleck, who had ordered them to wear uniform at all times and cancelled their weekly half-day off. I found a wonderfully wise CO who told me: 'Remember, your men are mercenaries. They will be as good as their officer.' (Shades of Kipling and the loyal oath to the Crown!) I found a second-in-command (nicknamed 'Trotsky') who advised me not to waste too much time learning Urdu because, really, Indian troops ought to learn English and, anyway, he found they understood perfectly if you shouted loudly enough (I did not make that up).

I was accorded a servant, the sixteen year-old grandson of the Mess head bearer, a young man who spoke English excellently and already knew exactly the morning ritual of bed tea, bath and trouser putting on. (A tricky athletic feat, this last, for the dressee).

A SOCIALIST SUBALTERN

I suppose nervous shock-waves should have agitated my socialist system to revolt. But I can only remember being amused, and often amazedly admiring—as of those young recruits from the villages, in scores of squads over acres of sunbaked parade grounds, marching, marching and marking time, in stages that took them week by week from coltish uncontrol to united precision as their senses succumbed to the central, insistent beat of the solitary drummer and his metronome.

I was too busy learning—learning to hear the rhythm of the language, to keep out of mule-kick at inspection time, to wrestle with unfamiliar names; too busy to pay homage to the storied screw-gun which frankly, to me, looked an insignificant peashooter after the guns I had been trained on in England. Then one day came an order to entrain for Madras. The train stopped three hours every day at stations, for officers to have their meals, and another two hours at spots out on the line, for the troops to have theirs. It took four and a half days to reach Madras and we had about fifty deserters on the way.

When the Japanese at last invaded Malaya, coming southward through what was then Siam, the forward defensive screen against them, up on the Malayan northeast frontier in Kedah, was formed by a company of the 1/14th Punjab Regiment. Supporting it were two 3.7 howitzers of the Sikh section of 4 (Hazara) Battery, FF, under the command of Second Lt. Knox. The Japanese reached the border in the early morning of 12 December 1941, and the first round we fired landed bang in the middle of the main road they were coming down. We had been surveying that road for months and we were rather pleased with ourselves.

The job of the 1/14th Company was to offer only enough resistance to enable us to estimate the Japanese strength, and then to fall back. In fact, 1/14th jawans began retreating through our gun position without warning very quickly indeed; also without their commanding officer, a Captain Mohan Singh. Mohan Singh had been an acquaintance before the fighting started. I knew he was disgruntled about a recent demotion, and I had some sympathy with him because I didn't think very much of one or two of the British officers in the 1/14th.

But I confess I hadn't expected to hear him, within a very few days, broadcasting from Radio Penang on behalf of the Indian National Army.

Thus, interestingly, if hazardously, began the long run from the Japanese down the 600-mile length of Malaya to Singapore. And in Singapore, on 15 February 1942, began three and a half years of prisonerdom, separated from the Indian soldiers I had commanded briefly, and not very efficiently, but with that real affection which kindles so easily in wartime that one is surprised how strongly it stays alight. Through the traceries of the grapevine we tried to keep some contact with our men, in or out of the INA. During those three and a half years I studied the progress of the Indian Independence movement with as much care as I could give it.

The change in the INA after Subhas Bose took over command was obvious even from behind our barbed wire. His claim that Hindu and Muslim soldiers were now eating in the same Messes was greeted with astonishment by old India hands. We talked about, sometimes with the Sikhs on guard over us, the 'Quit India' movement and its aftermath.

By the time I was freed and put on a ship back to India in 1945, I already felt that I knew a different country. The troop train from Calcutta to Ambala no longer stopped three hours a day for officers' meals. Catering was now properly organized and meals were handed into the coaches at certain selected stations. The train, however, ran increasingly late.

Foxtrot to Quickstep

Ambala was different too. When I had left the MATC, each day there had gone by as formal ritual, like an unswerving slow march, from the sunrise parade against the misty outlined backdrop of the far Himalayan foothills to the silver-sparkling dinner in the Mess, broken into a quick, submissive dissolution by the senior officer's retirement to bed. Now the days were like a variety of quick steps. 'Look,' said a young Sikh officer, just finding room in the crowded mess to sweep his 'made-up' pagri from his head.

'You never expected to see a Sikh do that, did you?' (He was right, though I didn't admit it.) And what he had under his hat, so to speak, was far more than a break with formal tradition; it was a whole new political library. Of that I had only time to catch a quick glimpse before I was ordered home to England and demobilization. But the brief introduction was enough to set up a persistently nagging curiosity to return.

After the war I went back to magazine journalism, this time in Ireland. The curiosity about India remained. My old orderly wrote to say that with the money I had given him he had acquired a 'bedfellow'. Then, in 1947, he sank without trace. Early in 1950 I asked the *Observer* if I might go to Delhi as their correspondent. To my surprise they agreed. In April I landed at Palam to be met by Evan Charlton, then Delhi news editor of the *Statesman*, who had been a good friend in Malaya and was then the only person I knew in Delhi. I felt very strange indeed; a new boy at the age of thirty-seven.

India is perhaps the easiest school in the world in which to lose first-term nerves. If a newspaperman is not always welcome (and it has to be said that there are times and places where he isn't) he is almost always, in India, made to feel welcome. I met the prime minister. I had tea, by administrative accident, two afternoons running at Rashtrapati Bhavan. Girija Shankar

Bajpai briefed me on foriegn policy, H.V.R. Iyengar on home affairs. Dr Matthai was the first of a succession of Indian finance ministers to go painstakingly over the country's economic problems with me. Even so I made some mistakes, though they were usually more of tact than of fact. I got quite a few things right as well. But I was still feeling my way around Delhi.

My wife had arrived, pregnant, with our two-and-a-half year old son, and took her sudden transition from her native Dublin to the start of a north Indian summer with amazing calm. She went up to Mussoorie where our daughter was to be born in September, and because she was there I made many trips to the hills. There was one time, early on, when I got a lift back in the car of a European diplomat. My fellow passenger was a Punjabi landlord. It was a hilarious journey and everything went wrong. And as the punctures and the hold-ups increased, and the meals failed to arrive and the sun got hotter, two companions became caricatures in their wrath, and somehow touched with caricature all the minor actors in the saga of our journey south. I wrote about the whole thing, and it really was rather funny.

A few days later, I was leaving the old Press Information Bureau in Raisina Road when I was stopped by Mohammed Subhan of the *Times of India*. 'You can't write things like that,' he said, referring to my *Observer* piece on the Mussoorie trip. 'Why not?' I asked. 'I'd write—indeed have written—the same kind of thing about England and Ireland.' 'But,' said Subhan, 'you know England and Ireland. You don't know India.' And I recalled what I felt when I had first arrived at Ambala; that I was too new to criticize.

Many years later, on that same road from Mussoorie—it was Independence Day, I remember, and the monsoon had just broken—I had a front tyre blown out. After a long skid the car, with myself, wife, two children and two dogs, left the road and went over the embankment. Miraculously no one was hurt, and within minutes a Punjab Transport lorry had pulled up on the roadside. The driver jumped out, inspected our vehicle, discovered the jack wouldn't work, organized the inevitable crowd of villagers to lift the car by hand, changed the wheel and drove the car, with villagers pushing, back up on to the road. The whole job took less than fifteen minutes and an offer of money was politely refused. I wrote that story too, thinking of Subhan the while.

NANDA DEVI TO KANYAKUMARI

But, back in 1950, I determined to get to know something of India by travelling. In Himachal Pradesh, Chief Commissioner Bhagwan Sahay showed me the physical (in the shape of road building) and political work being done in preparation for the first general elections of 1952. In Pondicherry R.K. Tandon, India's last 'foreign' representative before the French left, took me to Sri Aurobindo's ashram to meet the Mother. I searched for terrorists in Telengana with Special Commissioner Nanjappa, who later took me with him to do a puja.

I learned something of Hinduism from Dr K.N. Katju during an eclipse at Kurukshetra, and was given astrological guidelines by Professor B.V. Raman. I went on patrol with the Assam Rifles in Tripura and to my embarrassment found myself interpreting between a Madrasi captain and a Gurkha havildar. I reached Imphal a day before Pendril Moon was due to take over as Chief Commissioner there and, touring with the police chief, found myself mistakenly bombarded with petitions.

I toured Bihar in drought and flood and argued politics in Uttar Pradesh with the earliest of the Congress rebels and the first of the militant students. I travelled by train with Muslim emigrants from UP, through Rajasthan and up to the Sindh border of Pakistan. I was rioted around in Bombay, saw the fading days of Goa under the Portuguese and visited the old Indo-Tibetan trade fair at Rampur.

After the 1952 elections were over, my wife and I threw our two small children into the top berths of a railway carriage and set off for Bombay, stopping briefly en route at Bhopal where Khushwant Singh took us on a crazy and happily unsuccessful night search for tigers. From Bombay we went to Madras and thence to Bangalore, and finally via Trichinopoly to the toe of the subcontinent and across to Ceylon.

IT ONLY WEEPS

I travelled so much in those first two years because I thought I might never have another chance. But in fact during the next fifteen years I was seldom more than twelve months out of India and several times returned as a resident. Thus I saw three of the first four elections and the funerals of India's first two prime ministers. I covered the Chinese invasion of 1962, and the Rann of Kutch affair, and the Indo-Pakistan war of 1965. I was in and out of Kashmir as the fortunes of various politicians fluctuated there. I followed the Indian travels of Chou En-Lai, the Dalai and Panchen Lamas and Queen Elizabeth II. I saw the end of two great and reluctant rebels, Dr Ambedkar and Dr Shyama Prasad Mookerjee, as well as of that firm foundation stone of free India, Sardar Patel. Yet I'm not sure that any of the great names told me as much as a little old man in Mysore, in surroundings of torrential flood. 'It never rains in this country,' he said, 'it only weeps. And one waits until the morning to discover whether the tears are of joy or sorrow.'

Wherever I went in India, I was given quite extraordinary help by Indian journalists. Indeed I owe to them most of what success I may have had as a reporter. Khushwant Singh was Press Attache to Krishna Menon, then High Commissioner in London, when I set out to India for the *Observer*, and he began briefing me before I started. Prem Bhatia, before he was elevated to diplomacy, was always willing to share his wisdom. So was G.K. Reddy. In 1955 I shared a small hotel room with the two of them at the Bandung Conference, and kept them awake after their hard-working days by snoring all night. Otherwise, the arrangement was satisfactory. I typed for Prem and at G.K.'s request polished his English for him, and they briefed me on what Krishna Menon was telling them. George Verghese and Inder Malhotra have set me right on politics and economics; Sri Krishna opened up his library to me. Dilip Mukherjee, Subhash Chakravarty and Roy of UPI have tried to disentangle Bengali feuds for me, as has Ghosh of the *Statesman* whenever I was in Calcutta. And there are many more.

Even when I was outside India, Indians have often helped me. I shall not forget, just to take two instances, the hospitality of R.K. Nehru when he was ambassador in Cairo, or Girja Shankar Bajpai when he was in Pakistan. And those who have helped me have almost always taught me something as well. So you can see by now, I hope, what India meant to me. It meant a whole education, an open-ended education that will keep on proving me inquisitively ignorant until I die.

~

Rawle Knox came to India in 1941 after enlisting for service in the Second World War and was posted at the Mountain Artillery Training centre at Ambala. In 1950 he came back to India as a correspondent for *The Observer* Later, in the 1960s, he was roving Delhi correspondent for *The Daily Telegraph*.

XVIII

A Distant Involvement

~

SIR NORMAN KIPPING

I WRITE THIS ARTICLE with the certainty of being *sui generis*, for my career has not been in India and I have not lived or served there. Yet I have become involved with considerable parts of Indian industry and with its development and the problems of a developing nation: foreign knowhow against educated unemployment; reducing imports and increasing exports; establishing labour-intensive industries.

My work since 1946 has been with British industry, in the capacity of Director General of the Federation of British Industries—FBI (now transformed into the Confederation of British Industry—CBI). My responsibility was to promote the interests of its members, all of whom were manufacturers within the United Kingdom. For them, India was an important export market. A large part of Indian industries and all her utilities prior to her independence were British-based. They mostly used British machinery, even their technologies were of British origin.

Some large British companies (one thinks, for example, of Dunlop, Hindustan-Lever, ICI, British-American Tobacco) possessed important factories in India. Large parts of the

Indian cotton, jute, engineering, and coal-mining industries were run by British-owned managing agencies. Several British banks, insurance companies and shipping companies operated there. Nevertheless, for FBI members, India was an export market possessed, in the first post-war decade, of large sterling balances from which to pay for their imports.

TWO BIG CHANGES

Then came the First Five-Year Plan, with its concentration on building up India's heavy industries, especially steel. And, in the mid-1950s, two big changes in India's political position and one in her economic situation. The former was her decision to establish a great part of her developing industries in the public sector, and her position as a very large recipient of aid from the West and from Russia.

The latter—in the economic position—was the arrival of a serious and chronic scarcity of foreign currency. So India embarked on very rigid import controls and a policy of 'indigenization' of manufacture. All industries in India were put under great pressure to find ways and means of getting their supplies of machines and components from local sources.

So it quickly became clear to many British companies that had traditionally exported to India that there was only one way to keep that market—to manufacture within it. The period from 1955 to 1965 saw a wave of foreign investment in new modern factories in the private sector, most of which were developed jointly with Indian partners. In these developments, British investors have continued to dominate (some 45 per cent), although many have come from USA and from European countries, and a few since then from Japan.

Simultaneously, and under the same influences, Indian industries in which there was no (or very little) foreign investment have similarly expanded, obtaining their technology under agreement or by purchase from British or other foreign sources.

It was these developments that led to my deep personal concern with Indian affairs. The new British investors in the Indian private sector, and the participants in new technological agreements, were my FBI members. Their problems became my problems.

There were too obvious connections between British aid, the purposes to which it was applied and the rules governing its use, and British trade. I became firmly convinced that the best forms of aid were those which obviously served the interests of both lender and borrower.

In 1960, these two considerations led me to make proposals which resulted in a series of so-called Kipping loans, by which I am widely known in Indian industrial circles. This is the story of their origin.

With my interest in the well-being of British-based manufactures in India, I made a practice of visiting a great variety of factories there.

It gave me great satisfaction to see one splendid modern factory after another employing tens of thousands of Indians who otherwise would have been virtually unemployed and who were proving to be quick learners and adaptable people. But what I could not bear to see were these fine establishments constantly held up and working far below their proper efficiency because of shortages of spare parts, difficult components, small items of special materials or balancing machines. The shortages arose because of the cumbersome (though necessary) control of imports and because breakdown in production often cannot be foreseen. There was great trouble too in the system of stockholding of spares by established importers.

I became convinced that a scheme was needed to enable the management of factories, which were dependent on supplies from Britain of such bits and pieces, to take quick action in emergencies, without all the delays of queuing up for permits and licences. I worked out proposals for such a scheme and I suggested to the Government of India that, if they would adopt it, I would try to persuade the British government to finance it by an additional grant of aid. Fortunately I was successful and Kipping loans were born. The advantage to India is the high employment and productivity in her most modern factories. The advantage to Britain is that her overseas investments in these factories are more efficiently and therefore more profitably run. Thus mutual benefit results.

'INDIGENIZATION'

However, this is far from being the only problem in Indo-British industrial relations. In pursuing her policy of indigenization, India has been remarkably successful. Gradually, small Indian manufacturers have mastered the techniques and have progressively become reliable suppliers of specialized components. But indigenization alone has not solved India's chronic shortage of foreign exchange and her government has looked around for other ways of overcoming the difficulties.

Two ways, in particular, have emerged. One is the obvious objective of increasing India's own exports. The other is to attack the drain on foreign exchange which is represented by payments, in one form or another, for imported knowhow; that is, for technological agreements.

So far as exports are concerned, it is not far from the truth to say that every country in the world wants to reduce its imports and increase its exports. And almost every country possesses some natural advantages which give it export markets, such as is the case with Indian tea or Middle East oil or Russian timber. Nevertheless, the export of manufactured goods to the markets of the world is a highly competitive and sophisticated business, especially in 'high technology' goods. It involves skills in marketing as well as in production.

It is not enough for the Government of India merely to prod the Indian manufacturer or to threaten him with sanctions. It is necessary to identify the particular products and industries in which India enjoys advantages which will give her a lead over competitors. In labour-intensive industries, India's relatively low labour costs can provide this advantage. An example is the manufacture in India of components of the same design as are used in the home factories of foreign collaborators—for example, in the motor industry. But even in these cases, Indian companies will find that they have to accept rigid international standards.

The saving of foreign exchange in the purchase of know-how is even more difficult. It is very understandable that the Indian government, with 'educated unemployment' as one of its problems, should wish to see Indian companies doing far more research and development for themselves, rather than sitting back and leaving all this to the foreign collaborator. On the other hand, the foreign collaborator is in most cases years ahead with his R & D and, by centralizing these activities, is able to spend far more on them than could possibly be done by the Indian companies alone. Japan knows this well and, although she is a big and successful innovator, she remains a big importer of foreign knowhow. This then continues to be a problem.

My personal involvement in Indian affairs having thus been much more from outside than within, I have missed a great deal of India's infinite variety and the magnetic quality which so obviously draws those who have lived there. Ten visits of a month each, travelling far more to urban than to rural areas, though with some excursions into the latter, have been enough to teach me how little I know. But they have enabled me to meet many hundreds, perhaps thousands, in industries and banks and universities and government offices, in homes and in offices and while travelling, and to understand their aspirations and their daunting problems.

It has been an experience that has made me want to share a little in solving them. They say, and I think with truth, that British people who work in or with India leave a bit of their heart behind and bring away with them a bit of the heart of India.

~

SIR NORMAN KIPPING was an electrical engineer and industrialist closely associated with the Confederation of British Industry. In this role he was increasingly involved in the development of Indian industry and, in the 1960s, was renowned for a series of proposals which came to be known as the Kipping loans. He died in 1979.

XIX

From an Editorial Chair

~

EVAN CHARLTON

MY FAMILY HAS NO connection with India. I went there because the journalistic ladder in England in the mid-1930s was desperately overcrowded and I seemed to lack the right kind of technique for stepping on people's fingers to make my way up. I had learnt my trade thoroughly enough in the exacting school of local newspapers where accuracy is vital because you are living among the people you are writing about. After three years of it, however, I felt it was time to move on.

Fleet Street seemed unexcited by the prospect of employing me; so I answered an advertisement in the *Times* for a job in India. There were, I was told, some 200 other applicants and why the London agent of the *Statesman* selected me, I shall never understand, for he certainly gave no hint at our interview of regarding me with anything other than distaste. Perhaps all the others were scared off by the terms of the contract offered; five years, bound body and soul, starting at Rs 650 a month as a reporter/sub-editor. Perhaps they were put off by hints of the imperial responsibilities associated with working for so important a newspaper. Perhaps they did not care for indications that they would be expected to spend their spare time huntin', shootin' or fishin' but not, repeat not, poodle-fakin' which was the deliciously period term used for chasin' the girls.

LOW IN THE SOCIAL SCALE

Anyway, I brushed aside all apprehensions and, with thoughts of Kipling in my mind, I signed on. I soon found that the work of a sub-editor in the New Delhi office of the *Statesman* left precious little time for the sporting life and that the British caste system operating in India severely restricted the ordinary forms of girl chasin'. A young English journalist came so low down the social scale that only chaps who served in shops could be rated any lower. I did learn to ride, however, and on one or two occasions took part in the most exciting, most dangerous, blood-thirsty sport in the world: pig-sticking. I was petrified at the prospect of actually having to stick a pig and on one occasion, when a very angry boar came unexpectedly out of the sugarcane, my horse and I were equally frightened. The horse bucked high in the air; I fell out of sheer panic. What these expeditions did for me was to leave me passionately in love with the colours, patterns and smells of the great northern Indian plains.

It would be nice now to be able to claim that I approached my new life in India with a sense of dedication to the cause of Indian independence: nice, but quite untrue. On the other hand, I can say with a clear conscience that the idea that we (the British) should rule them (the Indians) indefinitely and in their own interests—which was at the time the prevailing British attitude—seemed to me to be totally unacceptable.

My attitude of mind can be traced to various factors. Next door to me at home in England had lived Dr P.C. Bhandari; he was a marvellously understanding doctor and he had become a close family friend. He was visited in his half-Indian, half-Western home by Pandit Nehru; he was in close touch with Mahatma Gandhi when he visited London. Once Dr Bhandari gave a lecture to the local branch of the British Legion which I reported for my newspaper; what his audiences of First World War veterans made of that lecture I never knew but for me it was a turning point. A country which could produce men like him hardly needed the British to run it for them. That view was swiftly reinforced by my personal observations in India.

In the office, I found my Indian colleagues journalistically able and personally agreeable but they had not advanced very far in their profession; the policy was to recruit young men like me to fill most of the key posts. There was little social contact in those days between Europeans and Indians on the informal, natural, friendly basis which is common today but what chances did come my way I took and greatly enjoyed. I was conscious that living an almost entirely European life meant missing the whole point of being in India.

When war broke out in 1939, it seemed to me that here was a chance for a major political rapprochement between the British and India. I have been seeing similar moments at intervals ever since but I have come now to think that perhaps my apolitical mind oversimplifies issues or overrates the human capacity for goodwill. Yet in 1939, all my Indian colleagues and friends were as firmly anti-fascist as they were properly patriotic; and we all waited for what we regarded as the inevitable declaration of the association of Britain and India in the war against Hitler's Germany, with the equally inevitable advance in Indian control of their own country. It did not come. Hope gave way to anger. I would have liked to come back to Britain; this was forbidden, despite the fact that my home leave was nearly due. Under the government's conscription rules, I stayed at my desk until I was permitted in 1941 to join the Indian Army. I was glad to go although dubious of my potentiality as an officer. New Delhi in wartime I found irksome.

No Political Animal

This is as good a point as any to make it clear that I am not in any way what is nowadays referred to as a political animal. I do, however, hold some strong convictions and if this sounds sententious, then it cannot be helped. There is Huguenot blood in my veins and there is Welsh blood. I went to a school of strong liberal tradition. Perhaps all these advantages contribute to my hatred of the oppression of one people by another, of a minority by a majority, of ruled by rulers. That is why I still regard the 1939 war as a just one and why I look back on the series of battles I fought with the Japanese with regret only for the fact that they were so dismally unsuccessful.

A sense of justice and an awareness of the individual dignity of man can only be sharpened and honed by years in India; the months I spent as a coolie building the Burma-Siam railway for the Japanese added to my deep conviction of the importance of concern for the individual. Once you have been part of a herd of helpless creatures, eating like hungry animals and sleeping and dying when exhausted, yet always aware of the preciousness of your own life to you if to nobody else, then it is impossible ever again to be unmoved by human suffering. But can political dogma ease the sufferings of the poor? Has political theory fed the hungry or housed the homeless? History to me speaks loud and clear. Such concepts are dangerous illusions; yet they continue to govern our lives.

That digression was not without purpose. I returned to India after the war in 1946, physically and mentally shaky but with a far greater awareness of human responsibilities than in the days of talk and gaiety in the fading 1930s. I watched the politicians cut up a country that could have retained its unity. Afterwards I learnt that I had been right at least on one fundamental point. The departure of the British was wholly beneficial in its effects; perhaps not least on those British who stayed behind. I continued to work for the *Statesman* in various capacities until my time as Editor came to an end in 1967.

To my great regret, I saw all too little of India outside Delhi and Calcutta but I had very little time for anything except my work. In fact, I now know that often I worked too hard but in the process I built up a store of interest, concern and knowledge which has left me with a curious personal sense of involvement in India which I wholly welcome—even if nobody else does.

It is this wider perspective on the world which I regard as India's most valuable gift to me. The more the people can see affairs other than through the blinkers of a belief in exclusive national virtue the better; this is one reason why I favour emigration and immigration and all the international schemes which involve people in working in countries other than their own. I am aware that this can and often does promote ill-will rather than goodwill. But the risk is worth taking, particularly at a time when an intense conviction of total national rectitude seems to be the stance of politicians everywhere. If, as sadly seems the case, universal man is on the retreat, India could do more than any other country in the world to stem the tide that is sweeping us back into our continental fortresses.

A foreigner in India has since Independence enjoyed remarkable opportunities. The majestic beauty of the scenery is matched by the kindness and hospitality of the people—to foreigners, at any rate, if not always to each other. Friendships are warm and durable and the easy pattern of social relationships is in sharp contrast to the cool, wary mingling in, say, England or France. Memory we know draws mercifully dark curtains across times of unhappiness and throws a brilliant spotlight on the moments of contentment. I can only remember once being treated with racial hostility the whole time I was in India, and that was by a minister who pretended to believe that a paragraph criticizing his ministry was written by me out of a sense of British superiority. The fact that I had not written the paragraph and would not tell him who had, only deepened his resentment. He faded from the political scene not long after this incident, convinced that the world was plotting his downfall. This, of course, is a common complaint among politicians the world over; an occupational health hazard.

That single incident apart, personally and professionally I found it possible to work as a journalist on a newspaper published in India with a sense of complete integrity of purpose and an awareness that what I was trying to do was generally understood and accepted. I was trying to produce a lively and readable paper, opening up new fields of interest for people to write about and giving scope to young men and women to express themselves and to help them to get on faster than it had been possible for me to do. I felt no need to wear a dhoti in Calcutta to demonstrate my affection for its inhabitants. In Delhi I did not don a Gandhi cap; the only firm order I have ever given to my wife was that she would not wear a sari in public. I came early to the conclusion that Indians share one somewhat disconcerting gift. They possess a sort of built-in radar which detects the phoney at first scanning. It is no good pretending that you adore Indian food if it cripples you; there is no point in pretending that you dote on Indian music if you cannot tell a tabla from a tomahawk. You fool nobody except yourself. Indians, I suspect, find foreigners who wax eloquently enthusiastic about all things Indian as irritating as I find foreigners who tell me that the British way of life is so much superior to everyone else's. Most people prefer candour to cant; the additional point to be made being that there is no need to equate candour with rudeness. We don't all have to be the same, think the same, behave the same. Differences make for interest.

The temptation to sentimentalize, to reminisce in an article like this must be resisted. What did India mean to me? A job I enjoyed, working with people I liked. Some minutes spent with some of the greatest men of this century. Some unforgettable sights, sounds and scents and the sharp awareness that I was a fortunate man to live through the times I did, see the changes that I saw and to be able now, on a cold spring day in London, to count up the names of at least a couple of dozen people as friends for our lifetime, even if we never meet again.

~

EVAN CHARLTON came to India in the mid-1930s as a reporter for *The Statesman* and was enlisted in the Indian Army in 1941 during the Second World War. He came back to India in 1946 and stayed till 1967, completing his stint as the last British editor of *The Statesman*. The now defunct, iconic youth magazine *Junior Statesman* (popularly known as *JS*) was his brainchild.

XX

Winds of Change

~

CEDRIC DAY

OLD VALUES AND VIEWS face a strong challenge ... and the pace of change will determine the future of the country.

India has been on the conscience and in the consciousness of the British for generations. India, in that sense, has always been with us—not merely in the popular image of heat and sunshine, vast crowds of people, elephants and cobras and holy men, maharajas in palaces and millions in huts, but in a more personal relationship.

Coming to India was therefore like returning to a familiar place and scene—but maybe this impression was the result of the brainwashing done by a wandering swami, who once had told me (for no reason at all) that in a previous reincarnation I had been a Hindu teacher; or perhaps it was because I, in my younger days, knew a number of Indian children in England and later associated with many Indians in London.

I have travelled to every state in India and have learnt that the diverse people have certain attributes in common: friendliness, kindness, courtesy, hospitality. This is true of the poor and the rich, the literate and the illiterate, the Hindu and the Christian, the Sikh and the Parsi—all of them.

This marked sense of hospitality can be a bit overwhelming,

as in the case of a charming couple I know. One day, innocently, I admired their bamboo screen and, before I could stop them, they sent it round to my house. Then, on occasions, there is the fun of being let into a conspiracy, as in a recent visit to some farmers in a Prohibition state. They insisted I must sample the wine they had made—not vintage but a treat to drink.

UNWANTED PURITANS

Mention of wine reminds me of the Prohibition sentiment expressed by some people. As one who firmly believes in the virtues of wine and other alcholic drinks and their social value when used in moderation, I find the prohibitionist a negative person. To ban drinking has as much chance of success as an attempt to ban sex—although I know there are some bleak souls who try to do both. One unfortunate outcome of prohibitionism anywhere in the world is that it promotes hypocrisy as well as disrespect for the law.

The strong streak of puritanism also induces some prudishness about sex. This is rather strange for a country which has produced the *Kamasutra* and a rich variety of erotic carvings in the temples. It seems to me that the joy of living expressed through the erotic of India is much to be preferred to, say, the sadhu's bed of nails. One has a feeling that the people who designed and built those temples and chiselled those vibrant figures had a fuller understanding of life, love and creation than those more austere descendants who build the small strawberry and vanilla temples of today.

The puritanical, negative side of Indian religions is as unattractive to me as the puritanical and negative aspects of Christianity, where the stress on sin and suffering and self-denial shuts out the warmth of love and brotherhood. But apart from the holy men and those who lean to the puritanical, I wonder how much faith the Indian masses have in their religions.

Perhaps that is not as important as it seems. Perhaps more important is the fun the people seem to have in the religious festivals. Whenever I have seen festivals, I have always come away with the feeling that the huge crowds have enjoyed themselves as though they had been at a carnival—a very happy and desirable state of affairs. Ritual bathing in the Ganga and immersing the images of gods and goddesses may be serious religious observances but they are also fun, which is something I didn't appreciate until I came here.

CHANGING VALUES

Patience, we were taught, is a virtue. After experiencing the seemingly endless patience of the people of India, I wonder whether one can have too much of a virtue. I think this same doubt is growing in the minds of the masses of India. Many of the traditional values and views are changing here; people are no longer content to accept that station in life 'to which it has pleased God' to call them. They want a change in the circumstances of life, they want more and better food, housing, education, clothes and other things. The apathy, so long a feature of the Indian masses, is going. What is yet to be determined is the pace of change—and this may well be vital to the future political stability of India.

Of course, there are people who are not interested in change, but, as I have gone around India, I have found the majority do want change. Let me give a few examples. About three years ago I was a member of a mission to Almora in

Uttar Pradesh, to see if the district would be suitable for a fertilizer project sponsored by the Federal Republic of Germany. We found the farmers and the extension workers clamouring for it. The project was established and the response of the farmers had been so excellent that the Germans are now expanding it to a multi-purpose scheme, introducing cattle, poultry, pigs, fruit, vegetables and so on—a development that will transform the area.

Again, recently, I was in Gujarat and saw a Freedom-from-Hunger Campaign project in one district where a canning plant had been established to grow a tomato crop—something they had never done before—and an excellent crop of tomatoes has just been delivered to the plant. In this and adjoining areas the farmers have also been persuaded during the past two years to grow fodder, something many predicted the Indian farmers would never do. Now more than 40,000, out of the 180,000 farmers in the area, are growing fodder.

A few months ago I was privileged to open the thirty-first Youth Club in a village in the Udaipur district of Rajasthan and there I saw a devoted team of extension officers from Udaipur University was helping to change the life of the villagers in the area, especially the young. Poultry-keeping, for example, is being taken up, mostly on a small scale, but I met one man who had set up a farm with 5000 birds. Breeding improved cattle and keeping kitchen gardens and fish ponds are other changes being introduced. And it is not only the villagers who are being changed. In one place I visited the director in charge and he told me he had spent several years abroad but had always stuck rigidly to his vegetarian diet. But now, convinced by his enthusiastic young team of workers, he had taken to eating eggs and poultry meat and, indeed, kept a flock of chickens to ensure a good supply of protein-rich food for his family.

EMERGING SCENE

I could multiply these examples a score of times but these are enough to illustrate my point that there is a ferment going on all over India. I have a feeling that we have been privileged to see the slowly emerging signs of the coming revolution of the Indian masses.

Finally, there is always something to interest and divert one in India. Recently, on emerging into the street, I met a bearded man dressed in loin-cloth and a ten-foot python which was coiled around him. He was holding the snake by the head and presented its open mouth and forked tongue to me—as though it was a 'mike' into which I was expected to speak. And then there is always the unexpected response. When an Indian member of our field staff was bitten by a cobra, I wrote to him in hospital, wishing him a speedy recovery, whereupon he replied he had indeed recovered due entirely to my good wishes. I hope the doctors didn't see his letter.

~

CEDRIC DAY was a bureaucrat who travelled extensively in India as a result of his various postings. He was associated with a number of development projects in the rural areas of Uttar Pradesh and Gujarat in the 1960s.

XXI

A Spacious Life

~

OSCAR H. BROWN

MY HOROSCOPE DECLARES THAT I would always be outspoken, blunt and forthright. I have found that this characteristic has served me well, if not wisely. Indians find the average Englishman horribly 'cagey'. In a railway journey, for instance, it does not take more than a few minutes for your neighbouring passenger to exchange his credentials with yours. It makes for a plesant journey and an immediate establishment of friendly relations. My countrymen prefer to be silent and are usually bores when travelling by plane, train or ship.

My early education was neglected because I was too young to go to a boarding school and too far from a kindergarten class. I first went to school at the age of eight and so missed the early companionship of fairies and fairytales. But by that age I was already a keen reader.

I won my first scholarship at Cathedral School, Bombay. I was a moderately good scholar, hopeless at mathematics, but with a good classical background. I felt it an iniquitous rule that one could not hold more than one scholarship at a time. I got this rule abolished thirty years later when I was Chairman of the Board of Governors of Cathedral School.

My abhorrence of geometry made me a candidate for the Cathedral Choir. Choir practice coincided with the geometry periods. I had a poor voice and failed to pass the test. However, when Dr Faulkner, the organist and choir master—large, musical and rotund—was in England on furlough and the choir was rather thin during the vacation, I became a choir boy to the discomfiture of Dr Faulkner, on his return. In my combative manner I remember telling him: 'I am in now and you cannot throw me out!'

Thomas Arthur Savage, headmaster of Cathedral School, was a fine Latin scholar. He also suffered from insomnia. For the Cambridge Senior Certificate, we had as our Latin prose text the *Twenty-first Book of Livy*, which narrates Hannibal's crossing of the Alps in his campaign against Rome. Livy tells us that Hannibal and his troops, wearing full pack, armour, greatcoats and heavy accoutrement, just lay down and went to sleep, fully dressed. The headmaster spent several minutes on praising Hannibal's ability to sleep fully dressed in military armour. From the back of the class I interrupted: 'But I can sleep fully dressed!' The headmaster was furious: 'So you are as great as Hannibal! Come here!' And I was duly flogged.

From Cathedral School I won a scholarship to St Xavier's College and was fortunate to come under the influence of two good and great Jesuits: Father Goodier and Father Hull. Father Goodier was principal of St Xavier's, an outstanding Shakespearean scholar and afterwards Archbishop of Bombay. He influenced my life at an impressionable age and gave me a sense of the right values which have shaped my subsequent career.

An unusual incident occurred at this time. Father Hull, an English Jesuit, was the editor of *Examiner*, a Catholic weekly which still flourishes in Bombay. Father Hull wrote a book on 'Love'—price: one rupee. Sixty years ago, youths in Bombay were not as sophisticated as they are today, I was essentially a scholar and knew little of the social accomplishments of youth. I could not perform a ballroom dance—I shuddered at the thought of putting my arm round a girl's waist. Believe it or not, at eighteen I had not kissed a girl! Now here came Father Hull's book. I imagined that it would introduce youth to the joys and ecstasies of love, I spent one rupee (then a heavy outlay) and bought the book. Imagine my dismay at finding it dealt with spiritual love and man's salvation.

I felt Father Hull had obtained one rupee from me by false pretences. I sat down and wrote him a four-page letter, accusing him of deception, fraud and several other misdemeanours. After a week I received a short note from him and an invitation to tea. I went and made the acquaintance of a fine scholar and a great gentleman. He was then in his fifties. I was eighteen. We had little in common but he went out of his way, gently but effectively, to correct my wholly mistaken and nebulous views on life. For the next twenty years he was my guide, philosopher and friend.

I took my degree in due course and was offered a post in St Xavier's College as a lecturer and simultaneously offered a vacancy at Cathedral School as an assistant master by Thomas Savage, a great headmaster by any standards. I went back to my old school.

I was a schoolmaster for some years and was being drawn to the Church. Then I met and fell in love with a beautiful girl who was also ambitious. Before accepting my offer of marriage, she made me promise two things: I was to renounce my intention of becoming a parson and I was to change the humdrum life of an ill-paid overworked junior schoolmaster for something more prosperous. And so I exchanged the Cap, Gown and Birch for the glitering prizes of the Bar. I was called to the Bar at Grays Inn, London, and returned to Bombay to practise as a barrister at Bombay High Court.

INDEFINABLE ATTRACTION

Why did I choose to return to India? It was the mysterious indefinable something which draws the Englishman to the country, apart from a family connection with India. I was reminded of it in 1947, when India became independent, and again in 1968, when I attended the Bombay Dinner in London. I met a host of friends I had known socially or worked with in Bombay. Without exception they all commended my decision to retire and settle in India. Many of them regretted they had done otherwise.

I have never thought of my friendship with Indians as being with people of another race. Their thoughts, words and actions have been as my own and I have never had any racial clashes with my Indian friends. I have always vigorously espoused their cause on every occasion. As an illustration, when the exclusive European clubs, of which I am one of the oldest members in Bombay, were thrown open to Indians, I rejoiced. I have found my Indian friends as clubbable as Englishmen.

I 'devilled' for many years in the chambers of D.F. Mulla, later the Rt Hon. Sir Dinshah Mulla, PC, a member of the Judicial Committee of the Privy Council. He was a great and good man. I owe him and his wife more than I have been able to repay. He was a very learned advocate and judge and a great and noble personality. It was indeed a great privilege to have learned the practice of law from such a giant.

I was offered a post on the magisterial bench by Sir Norman Kemp, the acting chief justice. I asked for time to consider. The independent life of a freelance barrister in Bombay has irresistible attractions and I hesitated to exchange it for the cold austerity and loneliness of the magisterial bench. Sir Dinshah thought differently and persuaded me to accept the offer. It completely altered my way of life but I have never regretted the decision. In eleven years, all my senior colleagues retired and I became Chief Presidency Magistrate and Revenue Judge of Bombay for the unusually long period of eleven years.

It was during my suburban days at Santa Cruz that I came to know Indarnarayan Brijmohanlal, later chief judge of the Court of Small Causes. He hailed from Delhi and had all the fine social talents of the Punjabi. He used to travel from Santa Cruz to Bombay by train and back. One day Indarnarayan almost missed the train. Seeing him run to catch it, I opened the door and he stepped in as I hauled in his huge mountain of flesh. He thanked me and we spoke to each other without any introduction. That helping hand brought me the best friend I had in Santa Cruz. He also lived there. Never a day passed without my visiting him or his calling on me. He had a voracious appetite. It was from him I learned to savour the rich and appetizing food of the Punjab.

Seasoned with Mercy

Once Indarnarayan had to decide a case against a man on the facts and law, but his sympathies were with the man against whom he had to pass a decree. He secretly sent the man a cheque for the amount of the decree he passed against him!

My career as Chief Magistrate was a soul-satisfying experience. On the very day I took my seat, I was welcomed by the Bar, and its esteem and affection I continued to enjoy during the whole of my judicial career——one of life's great rewards which I treasure.

In spite of the austerity and loneliness of the Bench and the fact that the chief magistrate is an overworked and underpaid judicial officer, it has great compensations. One gets an insight into the sordid side of life. Among the courts in Bombay, the juvenile courts are the most interesting.

I remember a curious case I tried in which a husband and wife of the poorer class quarrelled and the husband beat his wife while he was drunk. She was pregnant and had a fall. The child (a girl), when born prematurely, had a physical defect in one foot which, if not attended to early, would have led to lifelong lameness. As a result of their disagreement, the parents separated and, to maintain her child, the woman had to resort to a promiscuous way of life. The police arrested her for soliciting and took charge of the child, whom I remanded to custody at the Children's Home. I sent her to the J.J. Hospital and she was examined by a famous Indian surgeon (happily still alive), who gave a certificate that the foot could be put right by an operation if performed at once.

The arrest of the child brought the parents together and neither of them would consent to an operation to restore the child's foot. They were absolutely convinced that the child would die if she underwent an operation. The child was about five——a lovely girl with large beautiful eyes which gave promise of her blossoming into a fine young woman, if only her foot was restored to normal.

I was in a dilemma. The child's welfare demanded an operation, but no surgeon will operate on a child without the parent's consent. As the magistrate, I finally ruled that, in law, I was the guardian of the child while she was in judicial custody and gave permission in writing to the doctor to perform the operation. It was an entirely successful operation and, after convalescence, I restored the child (now completely sound and healthy) to the parents. They were now a happy united family. Every year, on the anniversary of the successful operation, they brought the child to the juvenile court for the remaining years that I presided in the juvenile court. On one occasion, the Home Member of the Government of Bombay was paying an informal visit to my Court when the happy family chose to call on me. The parent said: 'Sir, we have brought your child to see you.'

Imagine my chagrin and the utterly shocked countenance of the Home Member who was a dour Scot. The girl had now grown into a fine lass with a very glad eye. I explained the facts of the case to the Home Member but I don't think he believed me!

I held the inquiry into the Mahatma Gandhi murder case. The case was tried in Delhi in the Red Fort. For some reason, the accused were flown to Bombay and I was requested to hold the inquiry there. This included identification parades and the various incidents which lead up to the trial. I went to Delhi to give evidence at the trial of the accused. At the conclusion of my evidence, the accused handed me an autograph album with the signatures of the accused and their appreciation of the detachment and fairness with which the inquiry had been held. I treasure that book dearly.

VALUABLE LESSONS

Among the many outstanding members of the Bar who
appeared before me were Bhulabhai Desai, Coltman, Sir
Chimanlal Setalvad and Mohammed Ali Jinnah (a persuasive
advocate). I learnt much from them in the way of clear, lucid
argument. A patient judge is often better than a quick and
clever judge.

In 1947 I had to make an important decision. The Indian
Civil Service, Indian Police and other British civil officers,
including judges and magistrates, chose to leave India when
the transfer of political power from Britain to India was
effected. I elected to remain—though I was of British
nationality and British domicile. And I have never regretted
my decision.

Morarji Desai was then premier of Bombay and my relations
with him were most cordial. He was most appreciative of the
judicial work in the criminal courts and gave me generous
support. I could not have had a better executive head to work
with.

The Bar has always been hospitable to the Bench. The number
of festival occasions when the Bar has played host to the Bench
are legion. On Independence Day 1947, I insisted that the
Bench of the criminal courts should entertain the Bar. My
colleagues were surprised but heartily applauded my action as
an Englishman to unfurl the Indian tricolour at Esplanade
Court and the Bar thought it a fine gesture.

I became a member of the Bombay Philosophical Society,
which was founded by a small group of Professors of Philosophy
including Dr John Mackenzie, Principal of Wilson College,
Professor DeAndrade of Elphinstone College and Dr D.N.

Lawande. I was elected to the managing committee and, at the first meeting that I attended, I created trouble. My speech to the Committee was something like this: 'Come down from your high pedestal and bring philosophy from the Olympian heights down to earth. There are many young men in business and the professions who have acute minds accustomed to abstract thought but not yet skilled in the technical language of philosophy.'

Dr Mackenzie was convinced by my appeal and so the Bombay Philosophical Society now admits all shades of intellectual opinion and it serves the cause of philosophy in this state faithfully and well. For two years I was president of the Society.

SPORT AND PHILOSOPHY

I cannot think af a better companion on a holiday than Dr Lawande (Professor of Philosophy at Wilson College). I recollect a fine holiday we spent together in Kotagiri, where after golf we used to relax and his encyclopaedic mind would ramble on over Plato and Aristotle and the ancient Greeks. Life was good and satisfying when we could thus combine sport and philosophy in the rarefied atmosphere of the Nilgiri Hills.

My work has thrown me among Indians of every class, creed and colour and I have learnt much from them and learnt to love them. It may be because of my somewhat bluff and forthright manner. The Indian loves nothing better than a person who is free from any of the masks and protective armour of the silent, supposed strong Westerner.

I have received nothing but kindness during my long life

and work in India. I do not think there exists a race more appreciative and responsive than the Indians. Equally so are Indians sensitive to any attempt at being patronizing or arrogant. If I had to live my life all over again I would not alter my way of life by making a career in Europe. The prizes there may be greater, but India offers a more spacious life.

As the shadows lengthen and the evening of life sets in and the busy world slows down for me, I am satisfied that India gives me that peace at the last which I will not find elsewhere.

I have spent the happiest days of my life here. After a career as a schoolmaster, barrister and magistrate, I performed one final somersault (figuratively) in my declining years when I decided to enter Holy Orders at an age when other priests are retiring from the incumbencies. I find in the Church a chance of serving the people; of seeing life from still another point of view; and of making some contribution to others for the sum of human happiness, which India has given me in full measure, well pressed down and flowing over.

～

OSCAR H. BROWN lived in India from a young age, doing his schooling from Cathedral School, Bombay and his college from St Xavier's. He taught at the Cathedral School for some years before going on to study law. He was called to the Bar at Grays Inn but returned to India to practise as a barrister at the Bombay High Court.

XXII

Love and Hate

～

LIONEL FIELDEN

'I hated it (India) from the first moment and through all my five years there,' wrote Fielden. 'I never want to see it again.' This sahib may not appear to have loved India in the same way as the others but India meant a lot to him.

K.S.
14 February 1971

TO BE ASKED, AS I have been to write a brief article on, 'What India Meant to Me' is nearly impossible. It would need three books, India is a huge subcontinent of widely differing races: you cannot treat it—at least I cannot—as a single entity. In my book, *The Natural Bent*, I have described some of my experiences there. But to sum up briefly, what can I say? India gave me anger and depression, admiration and occasional pleasure, hard work and illness, frustration and despondency, and some very good Indian friends. And so on.

I think I must tell you the three silly reasons which made me come to India. The first was Eric Dunstan, the first famous 'golden-voiced' announcer of the BBC. A group of Indian businessmen, fired by the money-making success of the BBC, had built two inadequate stations in Bombay and Calcutta:

they knew nothing about broadcasting and soon went bankrupt. Eric Dunstan, for some inscrutable reason (since he was totally unfitted for such a job, though charming and talented), was sent out to remedy them. After a year he returned, a failure.

The Government of India, pressed by dealers, had to take over the stations: but it did so with ill-will, allowed them little money, and they went from bad to worse. But Eric had formed a passionate love of India, and talked to me at great length about its beauties. I began to want to go there. Second reason—rather worse—was that I was fed up with the BBC, which was turning into an institutional bureaucracy which I loathed. Third reason—even more silly perhaps—I was convinced that, given my head, I could make a better organization than the BBC. And India—illiterate India— seemed the perfect place for radio. When Willingdon, then Viceroy, decided that something must be done, I got the job and went to India, knowing almost nothing about it.

On my way to Marseilles to catch the boat I stayed for a few days with Aldous Huxley at Bandol. He said, 'You are absolutely mad: India is the most squalid and hateful country in the world and you will be miserable there.' If he was not quite right, he was not far wrong. I hated it from the first moment and through all my five years there. I never want to see it again.

FRIENDS AND ENEMIES

But do not get me wrong. You can't hate a place all the time for five years. I certainly hated the British Raj and its way, with the sole exceptions of Willingdon, Sir James and Lady Grigg and Lord Brabourne, whose premature death filled me with despair. Under his Viceroyalty I believe——still believe—— I could have made All India Radio a first-class institution. But Linlithgow was my enemy from first to last. After my first year in Delhi I avoided all British 'parties' and asked only Indians to my house. And thus I made enchanting friends: first Dr Husain, later to be, surprisingly, President of India, and then Mohammed Ali, most cultured and courteous of men; Radhakrishnan; and Minoo and Mehra Masani; Amrit Kaur; Sarojini Naidu; the beloved and beautiful Rama Rau family; and last but not least Rajagopalachari, the wisest and wittiest man in India, whose friendship I still keep with care. And I think I might even add Gandhi and Nehru whom I came to know well, and who were consistently kind to me. All these, and many more, were comforts. And of course I saw (briefly because I was seldom free) many beautiful places which I shall never forget.

In my five years in India we got fourteen well-equipped transmitters built, an admirable (though untrained) staff recruited for each, and employed 3000 artistes. I don't think it was a bad record as a foundation for a radio service and under the conditions. But only a foundation, and under awful conditions. The Government of India had the vile habit of snapping up all the money from licences and customs duties (the latter quite considerable) and then doling me out a sum which was about one-fifth of what was needed.

I protested and quarrelled and even wrote long articles for the *Times*, all to no avail. Therefore my staff and artists were grossly underpaid, our studios shabby and inadequate. After two and half years of grilling work I got ill: I had contracted tuberculosis though I did not know it at the time. I flew back for a month to England and on the plane met a soldier cousin and his wife, who thought, from the looks of me, that I would die on the way. My weight had fallen from eleven stone to eight. Well, I got somewhat better and returned but I knew that the game was lost. Despite everything I had done, All India Radio was returning into a stuffy bureaucracy, which could never make anything but mediocre programmes and, so far as I know, never has.

I hope you see what I am getting at. What India meant to me was certainly many good friends and lovely places, but also and, overridingly, poverty, apathy, indifference, and hideous overpopulation. So you see, my answer to the question 'What did India mean to you?' must be summed up in a single word— *frustration*. I wonder if it means the same to Mrs Gandhi today.

THE INDIA OF MY DREAMS

I should like to believe in a different destiny for India, a tapestry woven freely by Indian hands from the lovely varied thread of Indian differences and Indian history and Indian thoughts. I should like to think it possible that India could freely build her own way of life, rejecting the follies which have so manifestly brought Europe to disaster. I should like to see India, not pruned and rootless in the barren soil of materialism, but firmly rooted in her own ancient traditions, bringing from the past a measure of serenity and dignity to grace the graceless present. (From *Beggar My Neighbour*)

FIVE YEARS IN INDIA

The five years which I spent in India were, undoubtedly, the loneliest years of my life. The ache of loneliness was with me always. On the one hand there was the conglomeration of

English officials and their wives—the most ignorant, insensitive, arrogant, and. stupid conglomeration that the world has ever produced. During my first winter in Delhi, I went out to dinner with them almost every night. It was a terrible experience. Not only were their houses and furniture identical—they were built and supplied to the same pattern— but also the food, the guests, and the conversation were identical. There were always twelve people, and usually the same twelve. The dinner was always thin soup, wet fish, tasteless beef, and caramel custard. Since you were forced by etiquette to sit in an order determined by your salary, you sat almost always next to the same people. And, of course, you wore full evening dress. Very soon, I wanted to scream. The extraordinary thing was that any human being could stand it. Not a book was read or owned, in those trim, respectable bungalows: not a play had been seen: not a note of music was known: never was there even an echo of real laughter. In the similar roads with similar lamp-posts and similiar gates, it was as though one was shut up with a crowd of actors in an outdated pageant. It was a sad spectacle of third-rate tyranny.

(From *The Natural Bent*)

~

LIONEL FIELDEN worked for the BBC in London before coming to India as Controller of Broadcasting to the Government of India. He set up the All India Radio service and spent five years in India before going back to England in 1940. He authored two books—*Beggar My Neighbour* (1943), a study of the political situation in India, and an autobiography, *The Natural Bent* (1960). He died in 1974.